Fun Around the World for Preschoolers

Also in the Fun Around the World series written for first- through sixth-graders

Fun Around the World

More Fun Around the World

Fun Around the World for Preschoolers

Games, Art Ideas, Recipes, Songs, and More!

Compiled by Rhonda Reeves

new
hope
PUBLISHERS

Birmingham, Alabama

New Hope® Publishers
P. O. Box 12065
Birmingham, AL 35202-2065
www.newhopepubl.com

Dewey Decimal Classification: 793
Subject Headings: Games
              Multiculturalism
              Education, Preschool

ISBN: 1-56309-804-0
N048106 • 0204 • 5M

Dedication

To the writers of *First Steps in Missions*
Jennifer Cox
Brenda Morris
Beth Quick
Angie Quantrell
Kendra Thomason
Carolyn Tomlin
Tammie Worsham
Thank you for helping preschoolers to have
fun around the world!

Contents

Chapter
1

Fun Around the World for Preschoolers

In Angola

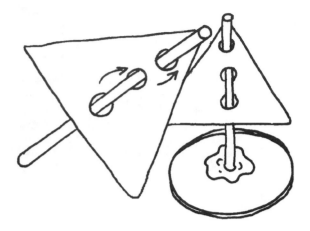

Simple Sailboat

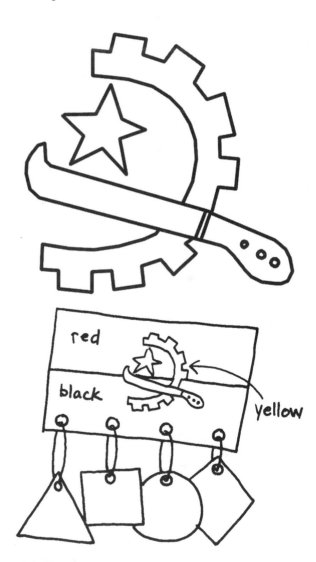

Flag of Angola

Angola

Simple Sailboat
Materials: wide, plastic lids; drinking straws; construction paper; scissors; hole punch; crayons; markers; stickers; clay

Help preschoolers cut triangles from construction paper to make sails. Encourage preschoolers to decorate their sails with crayons, markers, and/or stickers. Punch three holes along one side of each triangle sail. Guide preschoolers to weave a drinking straw through the holes. Put a small lump of clay on the inside of each plastic lid. Push the end of the drinking straw into the clay. Say: Angola has a long coastline and a beautiful beach. Four big cities have harbors where the boats come in and out of Angola.

Flag of Angola
Materials: 11-by-14 white paper; flag symbol pattern ; black, red, and yellow crayons; glue; yarn; construction paper; hole punch

In advance, enlarge and make one photocopy of the flag symbol pattern at left for each child.

Give each preschooler a piece of white paper with a horizontal line across the paper (long way). Lead preschoolers to color the top half of the paper red and the bottom half black. Help preschoolers color the photocopy of the half cogwheel, star, and machete yellow. Lead preschoolers to glue this design in the center of the flag. Say: This is the flag of Angola.

Angolan Houses
Materials: wooden blocks, people figures, toy vans

Encourage preschoolers to use blocks to build simple house structures. Say: In some parts of Angola, people live in houses with only two or three rooms. Sometimes 12 or 15 people live in the small house.

Provide people figures and toy vans to support play. Say: Many people ride in vans to get from one place to another.

Making Toys
Materials: variety of scrap materials (fabric, empty containers, wooden spools, film canisters, construction paper, etc.); scissors; glue; stapler and staples; yarn

Invite preschoolers to use the materials to make a toy. Say: Children in Angola do not have toys like yours. They often make toys out of trash. Could you make a toy using these things I have on the table?

Encourage preschoolers' attempts to be creative. Ask them to tell you about their original toy creation.
Teaching Tip: Be certain that none of the items provided have rough or sharp edges.

Wheel Book
Materials: Wheel Book Patterns, old magazines, glue, scissors, paper fasteners

In advance, enlarge and make a photocopy of the wheel book pattern and window wheel pattern at right for each preschooler.

Explain to preschoolers that many of the people in Angola do not have food to eat. Help preschoolers look through old magazines and cut out six pictures of healthy food items. Lead preschoolers to glue each of their pictures to one of the six sections on the wheel book pattern sheet. Say: I am thankful for food to eat.

Help preschoolers cut out the viewing window on the other pattern (cut on dotted lines only). Trim the edges of both wheels so that they fit evenly over each other. Place the window wheel on top of the picture wheel and punch a hole in the indicated place. Use a brad to attach the wheels. Show preschoolers how they can turn the top wheel to reveal each of their pictures underneath. Encourage preschoolers to name the foods they selected and glued on their wheels.

Digging for Diamonds, Mining for Gold
Materials: plastic container filled with sand, small rocks spray-painted gold and silver, plastic shovels or spoons

In advance, collect small rocks and spray paint them gold and silver to represent diamonds and gold. Hide them in the sand.

Invite preschoolers to find the "diamonds" and "gold" hidden in the sand by digging with the shovels and spoons. Say: Angola has gold and diamonds, but the people there are very poor.
Teaching Tip: Place a large vinyl tablecloth or piece of plastic under the table or plastic container to catch loose sand.

Rain Is Coming!
Materials: rain boots, umbrellas (with plastic safety tips and no-pinch openings), raincoat, rain hats, assortment of other clothing choices, audio recording of rain or thunderstorm

Say: Angola has a rainy season when the streets are flooded with rain. Let's pretend we are getting ready for a rainy day. What would we wear?

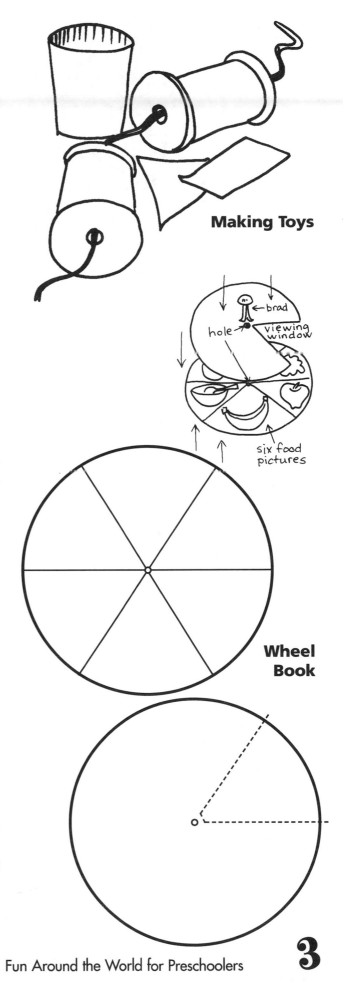

Making Toys

Wheel Book

Caring for Babies

Beach Treasures

Ocean in a Bottle

Play the recording, and help preschoolers sort the clothing articles to decide which ones would be appropriate for a thunderstorm or rainy day.
Caution: Supervise carefully when using an umbrella.

Caring for Babies

Materials: baby dolls; large pieces of fabric; doll play props (diapers, bibs, etc.)

Explain to preschoolers that people in Angola wear large pieces of material, called panos, wrapped around their bodies. The women also use the panos to carry their babies on their backs. Help preschoolers wrap the fabric around their bodies to resemble the panos. Encourage preschoolers to pretend to carry their babies on their backs using the panos.

Beach Treasures

Materials: plastic tub filled with play sand, shells, starfish, sand dollars, other beach items, plastic shovel(s)

Hide the shells and beach items in the sand. Invite preschoolers to dig through the sand to find the hidden items. Say: Angola is a country near the ocean that has beautiful beaches.

Ocean in a Bottle

Materials: clean, empty 2-liter bottle; water; oil; blue food coloring; small shells; glitter; nature items from the beach (seashells, sand dollars, starfish, etc.)

In advance, fill a clean, empty 2-liter bottle with water and oil. Add a few drops of blue food coloring, along with some glitter and small seashells. Place the lid on the bottle. Secure with heavy tape, or hot glue the lid on the bottle so preschoolers can't open it.

Shake the bottle and ask preschoolers what they see. Explain that Angola has beaches with shells and water. Assist preschoolers in holding and exploring the ocean in a bottle.

Chapter 2

Fun Around the World for Preschoolers

On the Arabian Peninsula

The Arabian Peninsula

Bottled Sand Art

Materials: baby food jars or any other small jars, colored sand, uncooked spaghetti pasta, teaspoons

Lead preschoolers to spoon three or four layers of colored sand in their jars. When filled to the top, give each preschooler a piece of spaghetti. Guide them to poke the spaghetti through the sand in several different places next to the sides of the jar to make pretty designs. Say: Much of the Arabian Peninsula is made of sand.

Teaching Tip: In another area of the room away from preschoolers, have a hot glue gun to glue the lids onto the jars.

Caution: Supervise preschoolers carefully when using the hot glue gun.

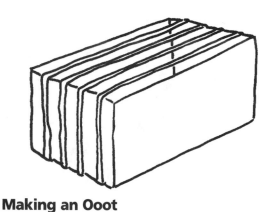

Bottled Sand Art

Making an Ooot

FYI: An *ooot* is a four-stringed guitar type instrument played in the Arabian Peninsula.

Provide a small shoe box (no lid) and four rubber bands of varying widths for each preschooler. Guide preschoolers to place their rubber bands over their shoe boxes lengthwise. Lead preschoolers to "strum" or "pick" their *ooots*.

Making an Ooot

Basket of Balls

Place one or two laundry baskets full of various sizes of balls in the area. Include a soccer ball. Say: Children in the Arabian Peninsula like to play with balls. Soccer is their favorite game.

Tent Play

Provide a tent for preschoolers to play in. If one is not available, use a sheet to throw over a table. Provide small area rugs to place inside. Say: Some Arabian families take tents to the desert and have picnics.

Pitas

Materials: pita bread; jam; cheese; small paper plates; napkins; allergy alert chart, page 93

Say: The people of the Arabian peninsula eat *xhubs*, the original pita bread, usually with jam or cheese.

Encourage preschoolers to make their own *xhubs*.

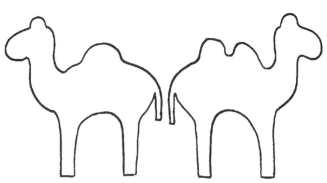

One Hump or Two?

One Hump or Two?

Photocopy the pictures of camels at left. Cut out camels and glue to the end of tongue depressors. Cover two tin cans with paper and write the numeral one on the first and the numeral two on the second. Lead preschoolers to place the camels in the correct can.

Say: Camels are used for travel in the Arabian Peninsula. You can see people riding them even in the cities.

Chapter 3

Fun Around the World for Preschoolers

In The Balkans

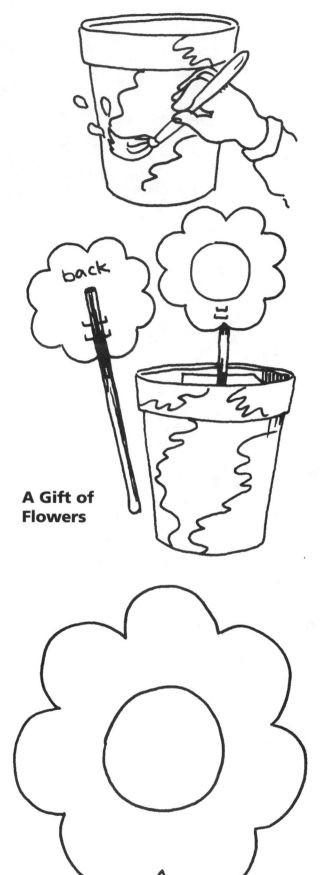

A Gift of Flowers

The Balkans

A Gift of Flowers
Materials: small clay flowerpots, Styrofoam, paints, brushes, plastic drinking straws, photocopies on construction paper of the flower pattern at lower left, stapler, staples

Guide preschoolers to paint their flowerpots with the paints provided. While the pots are drying, help preschoolers cut out a flower pattern. Staple the flower to the end of a plastic drinking straw. Lead preschoolers to place a piece of Styrofoam into the bottom of the flowerpot, and then push the straw into the Styrofoam until it stands. Add artificial grass to cover the Styrofoam. Say: Many beautiful flowers grow in the Balkan states. Many times people give flowers as a gift when they are invited into someone's home.
Teaching Tip: An adult should operate the stapler to avoid injuries.

Lace-and-Doilies Collage
Materials: construction paper, glue, scissors, lace remnants, paper doilies, handmade doilies and lacework

Provide a variety of paper doilies and lace remnants and lead preschoolers to create a collage using the available materials. Say: The people of the Balkans enjoy making doilies and lace to decorate their homes.

Mountain Hike
In advance, find the following items: map, backpack, boots, hiking and backpacking equipment (rope, canteen, lantern, etc.).

Tell preschoolers that mountains are in the Balkans. Most are covered with thick forests. The people of the Balkans like to hike, explore caves, and go backpacking.

Guide preschoolers to pretend to put on hiking boots and prepare for a hike up the mountain. Remind preschoolers to put on their backpacks and gather up their gear. Ask them what they might see along the mountain trail. Pretend to climb the mountain as you walk with preschoolers around the room. When you get to the end of your mountain hike, you might want to provide cups of water or a simple snack.
Caution: Be sure to post the allergy alert chart (p. 93) if serving a snack.

A Croatian Meal

Materials: broth or soup, cheese, hard crusted white bread, apples, plates, napkins, plastic utensils, allergy alert chart (p. 93)

In advance, display the chart to alert parents and families concerning this activity.

Invite preschoolers to prepare a typical Croatian dinner including soup, cheese, white bread, and apples. Encourage preschoolers to serve themselves. Remind them to speak politely to one another, using words such as please and thank you. Say: In Croatia soup and cheese are served every meal—even breakfast!

Over Walks and Cows

Materials: transportation theme rug or floor mat, toy vehicles, blocks, plastic toy cows, people figures

Tell preschoolers that many of the busy roads in the Balkans are too dangerous for people to cross. Over walks are built above the highways. Sometimes people walk over the highways on these bridges. Sometimes they even lead their cows across the over walks so they will safely cross the street.

Lead preschoolers to build a busy highway and then construct a walkway over the highway. Pretend that people and cows are walking over the busy highway using the over walk or bridge.

Over Walks and Cows

The Coffee Shop

Materials: coffee pot, coffee mugs, tables, chairs

Say: In the Balkans, people enjoy talking and spending time with friends. They like to drink coffee together.

Encourage preschoolers to role-play pouring and drinking coffee. You might provide ground coffee for preschoolers to smell and feel.

Foods to Explore

Materials: lemons, tangerines, kiwis, olives, plastic knives, napkins, plates

In advance, post the allergy alert chart (p. 93).

Show preschoolers the items. Say: These foods grow in the Balkans. Do you know what each one is called?

Help preschoolers identify each item and describe it. Lead preschoolers to taste each item.

The Coffee Shop

Ice-Cream Book

What Makes a Forest?

Materials: tree leaves and branches, tree bark, toothpicks, paper, wooden block, section of tree trunk, magnifying lens

Lead preschoolers to examine the items with the magnifying lens. Say: Many trees and forests are in the mountains of the Balkans.

Ice-Cream Book

Materials: ice cream and cone patterns at left, hook-and-loop fastener, markers or crayons, glue, 4 pieces of manila paper

In advance, make four copies of each pattern. Cut out the cones and glue one to each piece of paper. Underneath the ice-cream cone, print a color word, such as *brown, pink, green,* or *yellow.* Print the word using a marker of that color. Trace the ice-cream scoop patterns onto construction paper using the same colors of paper as suggested on each page. Laminate the "scoops" for durability. Trim excess plastic. Attach the loop side of the fastener to the back of each scoop. Place the hook side of the fastener above each cone.

Lead preschoolers to match the correct ice-cream scoop to the corresponding color page. Help preschoolers attach the scoops to the cones. Say: Croatia has many ice-cream shops. They serve homemade ice cream in 10 to 20 flavors. The ice-cream shops are called slasticarnice [sla-tee-char-neet-sa].

Sailboats on the Water

Materials: plastic tub filled with water, blue food coloring, toy plastic sailboats

Say: The waters of the Adriatic Sea and the Mediterranean Sea are a beautiful blue. The people of the Balkans enjoy boating on the water.

Place a few drops of blue food coloring into the water and observe what happens. Ask preschoolers what might happen if the boat moved around on the water. Experiment and find out.

The Pen Game

Provide a variety of ballpoint pens. Help preschoolers count the pens, make patterns with the pens, sort the pens by color, place the tops on the pens, etc. Ask preschoolers to think of ways to use the pens. Hide the pens and lead preschoolers to find them. Say: The ballpoint pen is something we use all the time. It was invented in Croatia, one of the Balkan states.

Chapter

4

Fun Around the World for Preschoolers

In Bolivia

Bolivia

Clay Huts
Materials: clay; clay tools (plastic knives, craft sticks, rolling pins); dried grass, sticks

Provide the materials for preschoolers to create a mud hut. Guide them to create thatch roofs with the dried grass. Say: In Bolivia many of the houses have thatch roofs. Some of the churches have thatch roofs and no walls. Can you think of a way to build a church with a roof but not walls? The huts and churches in Bolivia are made from clay or other materials the people can find.

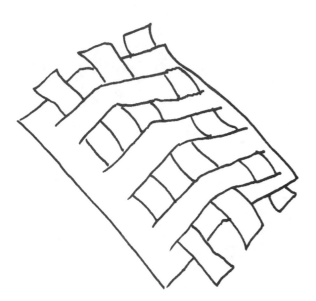

Paper Weaving

Paper Weaving
Materials: 12-by-18 inch construction paper, scissors, tape

In advance, fold sheets of construction paper in half, widthwise. Starting on the folded edge, cut lines 1½ inches apart, stopping 1½ inches from the open edge. Unfold the construction paper. From other sheets of construction paper, cut 1½-inch strips.

Guide preschoolers to weave the strips in and out of the large piece of construction paper with cuts. Tape the ends of the strips to prevent them from falling out. Say: People in Bolivia like to weave and spin. They have colorful blankets!

Along the Dirt Road
Materials: plastic container filled with dirt, plastic toy pigs and sheep, toy cars and tractors, blocks

Guide preschoolers to use the blocks to build a village in the dirt. As they work, say: Many of the Bolivian people travel on rugged, dirt roads. Some of them have cars and tractors. Sometime pigs and sheep roam the roads until the owner calls the animals and herds them back.

Along the Dirt Road

Building a Mountain
Materials: cardboard blocks or soft foam blocks, large green towel or blanket, toy vehicles

Suggest that preschoolers stack the blocks to build a mountain. Cover it with a green towel or blanket. Lead preschoolers to pretend to drive the cars over the mountain. Say: Bolivia has beautiful mountains.

Open-Air Market
Materials: colorful woven cloths and blankets, plastic fruits and vegetables, play money, tables

In advance, prepare an area to resemble an open-air market with booths or tables where goods, fruits, and vegetables are bought and sold. Support preschoolers' play as they pretend to buy and sell goods at the market. Say: In Bolivia, the people often shop in an open-air market.

Teaching Tip: Encourage preschoolers to name the fruits and vegetables displayed in your market.

Animal Counting Book

Materials: construction paper, rain forest animal stickers, stapler, staples

In advance, make a construction-paper book. Apply stickers so that page one has one sticker, page two has two stickers, and so on. Stack the pages and staple them together.

As preschoolers read the book with an adult, encourage them to count the number of animals on each page. Say: Many beautiful and different animals live in Bolivia.

Animal Counting Book

Arroz con Leche

Materials: ½ cup rice, 1 quart milk, cinnamon sticks, ½ cup sugar

In advance, post the allergy alert chart (p. 93) to notify parents of this cooking and tasting activity. Wash the rice, and let it soak in the milk for one hour.

Lead preschoolers to help prepare rice and milk *Arroz con leche* [ah-ROSE cohn LEH-cheh]. Cook it over low heat with the cinnamon sticks until it thickens. Stop cooking and add the sugar. Serve hot or cold. Say: Many of the people in Bolivia are very poor. They eat rice and potatoes every day. This is one way they cook rice. Bolivians often cook in outdoor kitchens.

Note: This recipe serves five people. Give each child a plastic spoon filled with a sample taste.

Tropical Fruit Salad

Materials: large plastic mixing bowl; mixing spoon; paper cups; plastic spoons; napkins; tropical fruits (banana, coconut, grapefruit, mango, orange, papaya, passion fruit, pineapple, tangerine)

In advance, post the allergy alert chart (p. 93) to notify parents of this tasting activity.

Tell preschoolers the names of each fruit. Say: These are all tropical fruits that you might find in Bolivia. Who would like to help me make a fruit salad?

Encourage preschoolers to mix fruits together, stir the mixture, and serve it into paper cups. Provide a plastic spoon for preschoolers to taste their tropical salad.

Tropical Fruit Salad

Smell the Rain Forest

Smell the Rain Forest
Materials: empty film canisters; cloth squares; tropical products (cloves, nutmeg, black pepper, lemon peel, pineapple, chocolate, avocado, banana, coconut, grapefruit, guava, lime peel, mango, orange); rubber bands

In advance, put a sample of a fragrant tropical item into the canister and cover it with a small piece of cloth. Secure the cloth with a rubber band. Place the cap on the canister.

Invite interested preschoolers to smell the concealed item in each canister and guess what it might be. After the preschoolers guess what the smells are, show them what's in each canister. Say: These are all products from the tropical rain forest.
Note: Semitropical rain forests are in Bolivia.

Bolivian Games
Help preschoolers kick or play with a soccer ball in a well-defined space or outdoors. Teach older preschoolers how to play marbles. Say: Children in Bolivia enjoy playing soccer and marbles.
Teaching Tip: Supervise carefully to be certain preschoolers do not place marbles in their mouths or noses.

Water Play

Water Play
Materials: water table or large plastic container filled with water; variety of water toys (sieve, funnel, boat, plastic alligators and turtles)

Lead preschoolers to play in the water. Say: Bolivia has beautiful waterfalls. Can you make a waterfall? Alligators and turtles live in Bolivia. Rivers are in Bolivia, too. The water is not clean to drink.
Caution: Supervise carefully.

Animal Scavenger Hunt
Materials: photographs of animals, including jaguar, parrot, monkey, anteater, turtle, and alligator

In advance, hide photographs of these animals around the room.

Tell preschoolers that some of the animals found in Bolivia have escaped from the rain forest. Ask them to be good detectives, and help you search for them. After the animal photos have been found, gather preschoolers and show each photo. Help them identify the animal depicted.

Chapter
5

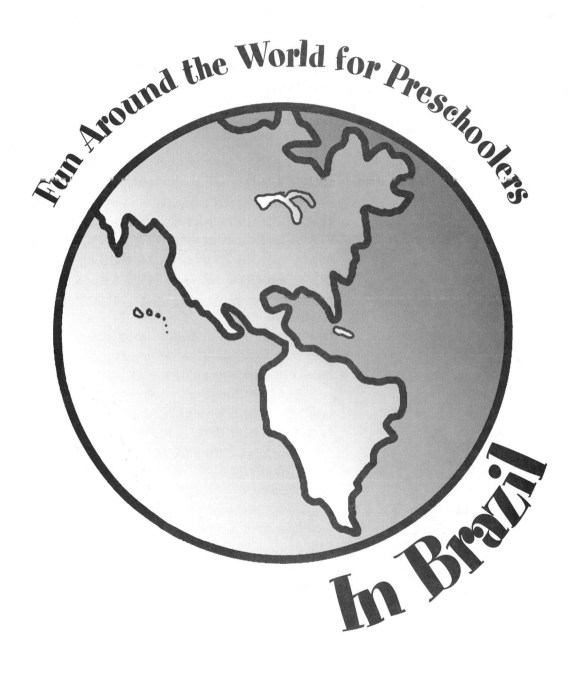

Fun Around the World for Preschoolers

In Brazil

Brazil

Dude-Ranch Floor Mat

Materials: large piece of butcher paper, markers, blue and green paint, brushes, aprons, picture of a ranch

Show the picture. Guide preschoolers to draw a dude ranch. Suggest they draw green hills and blue rivers also. Encourage them to paint the scenery. When dry, use markers to add a barn, a house, pastures for horses, fences, and roads. Add toy horses and blocks. Say: Many people in southern Brazil ride horses.

Pastel Houses

Materials: white construction paper, oil pastels, 1-inch squares cut from brown construction paper, glue

Invite preschoolers to draw houses with the pastels. Help them put doors and windows on their houses. Glue tiles on the roof (square papers). Say: Many houses in Brazil are made with painted bricks and tile roofs.

Horse Racing

Materials: plastic horses and cows, trucks with trailers, fences, 1-yard lengths of rope, picture of cowboys roping cattle and horses racing

Help preschoolers make racetracks and corrals with the rope pieces. Race the horses to see who is fastest. Pretend to rope cattle and load them onto a truck. Say: Some people in southern Brazil are called gaúchos [gah-OO-shoes], or cowboys. The gaúchos ride horses and herd cattle.

Horses and Carts

Materials: plastic horses, string, scissors, masking tape, small boxes (jewelry or pudding)

Show how to make a horse and cart with a box and string. Help cut a long piece of string and wrap the center around the horse. Tape the two ends to a box, one on each side. Show how to move the horse along the floor, dragging the cart. Provide small blocks and see how much the horse can pull. Say: In Brazil you can see horses and two-wheeled carts in town. The carts drive right beside cars and buses.

Pastel Houses

Horses and Carts

Bottle Bowling

In advance, fill six empty 2-liter soda bottles three-fourths full of water. Drop several drops of food coloring in each. Tightly close the lids. Set up like a bowling lane formation.

Give preschoolers a soccer ball, and let them bowl down the bottles. Say: *Gaúchos* play a game called *bocchi* [BAH-shee] ball, which is an Italian version of bowling.

Farms and Tractors

Materials: toy tractors, trucks, and farm equipment; toy barn; tub filled with 2 inches of soil; sheet

Spread the sheet on the floor, and place the tub in the center. Suggest preschoolers farm the dirt with farm equipment. Say: Farmers in Brazil grow many things, such as coffee, bananas, lemons, cacao beans, oranges, and pineapple. They grow food for the people to eat.

Bottle Bowling

Gaúcho Clothes

Materials: bandanas, cowboy hats with chin straps, bolo tie, cowboy boots, vests, stick horse, short pieces of soft rope (2 feet long), picture of a *gaúcho*, toy guitar, mirror

Show the picture of the *gaúcho,* and invite preschoolers to dress up like a *gaúcho.* Suggest preschoolers look in the mirror. Encourage them to ride the stick horse. Say: Many people in southern Brazil are called *gaúchos* [gah-OO-shoes]. They ride horses and herd cattle. Guitar music is popular in Brazil.

Make a Waterfall

Materials: plastic tub on a towel on the floor, pitcher of water, flat stones, waterfall picture

Show how to stack the stones to make a tower. Create a waterfall by gently pouring water on the top rock, letting it cascade down. Let preschoolers make their own waterfall. Say: The Iguacu [ee-gwah-SOO] Falls are in Brazil. It is the biggest waterfall in the world.

Teatime

Materials: tea set including cups, saucers, teapot; diluted tea; sugar; toy bread, cake, fruit; plates

Pretend that preschoolers are school children who just got home from school. Serve them tea,

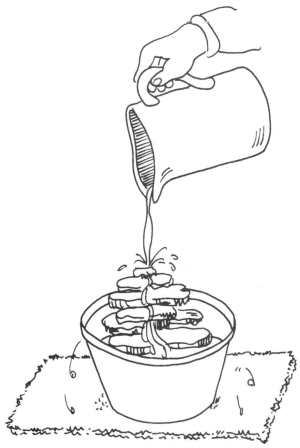

Make a Waterfall

Coffee Grounds

and a snack of bread, cake, or fruit. Say: Boys and girls in Brazil have a teatime after school. Most families send their preschoolers to school.

Coffee Grounds
In advance, save a pound of used coffee grounds. Spread wet grounds on paper towels on a cookie sheet to dry. Save. Place the grounds in a large bowl on a table, and place spoons and plastic coffee cups nearby.

Invite preschoolers to smell, touch, and scoop the coffee into cups. Say: Brazil grows lots of coffee beans. Everybody drinks coffee, even boys and girls. The boys and girls have it with milk and sugar.

Chapter
6

Fun Around the World for Preschoolers

In Burkina Faso

Burkina Faso

Dying Fabric

Materials: light colors of fabric scraps about the size of a paper towel, construction paper, three containers of thin tempera paint, paint smocks, newspaper, glue

In advance, cover a work area with newspaper. Prepare three colors of tempera paint. Cut fabric in several sizes.

Place a smock on each child. Show preschoolers how to fold the fabric in different ways. Next suggest they dip the fabric in a variety of ways into the paint. (This procedure will make different patterns.) Lead preschoolers to unfold the dyed fabric carefully and put it aside to dry. Show preschoolers how to glue the dye art on a contrasting color of construction paper.

Say: The people in Burkina Faso use berries from plants to make dye.

Basket Weaving

Materials: construction paper, pictures or stickers of fruit and vegetables, glue, scissors

In advance, cut basket shapes by folding a 9-by-12 piece of construction paper in half. Cut slits in the basket shape. Cut construction paper into 1-inch wide strips. Cut out pictures of fruit and vegetables.

Guide preschoolers to weave paper strips through the slits on the basket. Glue the finished basket onto a piece of 12-by-18 construction paper. Invite preschoolers to fill the basket by gluing on pictures or stickers of fruits and vegetables. Say: In Burkina Faso, some women take baskets to the market. When they have finished their shopping, they put the baskets of food on their heads and walk back home.

Basket Weaving

Mud Bricks

Materials: clean dirt, sand table or dishpan, bucket, water, garden spades, smocks, cookie sheet, paper towels

In advance, fill the sand table or pan with clean dirt (top soil that has been sifted of rocks and plants and had boiling water poured through it).

Guide preschoolers to wear smocks. They pour water into the dirt until the mixture is a clay-like consistency. Lead them to use hands and garden spades to mix and shape the mud into bricks or other shapes. Place finished products on a cookie sheet to dry. Say: In Burkina Faso people make mud bricks. When the bricks are hard, they are used to build houses.

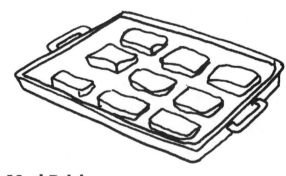

Mud Bricks

Teaching Tip: Clean mud from preschoolers' hands and arms in the bucket of water, then wash hands at the sink with soap.

Learning to Read
Materials: small slate boards, chalk, clear plastic report covers, erasable marker

As a child draws on the slate board or plastic cover, say: Many of the people in Burkina Faso do not know how to read.

African Dress
Materials: pieces of bright printed fabric that will wrap around a preschooler, baby dolls, pictures of African people in traditional dress, baskets

Show how mothers in Burkina Faso carry the babies on their backs while they are working or shopping. Help the girls wrap a piece of fabric so that they can carry the baby doll on their backs. Also help boys and girls to walk with a basket of lightweight items on their heads.

Sing the following to the tune "Here We Go 'Round the Mulberry Bush":

This is the way we carry the baby, carry the baby, carry the baby.
This is the way we carry the baby
All through the village.
Continue with other verses that include:
This is the way we carry the water.
This is the way we carry the food.

African Dress

If You Lived in Africa
Lead boys and girls to walk around in a circle to the beat of a drum, singing to the tune "The Farmer in the Dell":

Oh, if you lived in Africa,
Oh, if you lived in Africa,
If you lived in Africa,
Oh, what would you do?

When the drum beat stops, a child tells what she would do if she lived in Africa. Continue giving others a turn to answer and to beat the drum.

Kick the Stone
Materials: beanbag, box, carpet square, other things preschoolers can kick the beanbag in or on

Give instructions to kick the beanbag into the box, on the carpet square, off the carpet square, etc. Say: Many of the boys and girls in Burkina Faso do not

If You Lived in Africa

have toys and games. They like to play tag, and some make toys from scrap materials. Some of the boys will kick small round stones when they are outside.

Out in the Bush
Lead preschoolers to do the motions pictured as you chant:

Out into the bush we go.
(Preschoolers bend low, making swishing sounds as they go through the bushes.)
Out into the bush to see what we can see.
(Boys and girls hold a hand up to their forehead as they look all around.)
Out into the bush we go, Sh, sh, what did I hear?
(Everyone stops, cups hand to his ear as they listen.)
Out in the bush I hear an elephant.
(Make sounds like an elephant coming through the bush.)
Be very quiet!
(Stand still as can be while the elephant goes by.)
Out in the bush we go to see what we can see.
Continue adding other animals and actions.

African Scenes
Find pictures of African scenes and mount on sturdy cardboard. Laminate for durability. Cut each scene into 6 to 12 pieces. (The number of pieces will depend on the age of your preschoolers.) Younger preschoolers will need fewer pieces. Lead preschoolers to put the African scenes together.

Store puzzle pieces in a plastic self-sealing bag until ready to use.

Raindrops Are Falling
Materials: paper, several medicine droppers, blue food coloring, water, waxed paper, newspaper

Guide each child to lay a sheet of waxed paper on the table. He uses the dropper to pick up some of the blue water. He then drips water onto the waxed paper. Drop another drop on top of the first drop. He continues adding drops of "rain" until a small puddle is formed.

Say: Some months so much rain falls in Burkina Faso that it makes lots of big puddles on the ground.

Out in the Bush

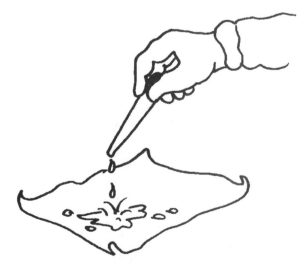

Raindrops Are Falling

Chapter 7

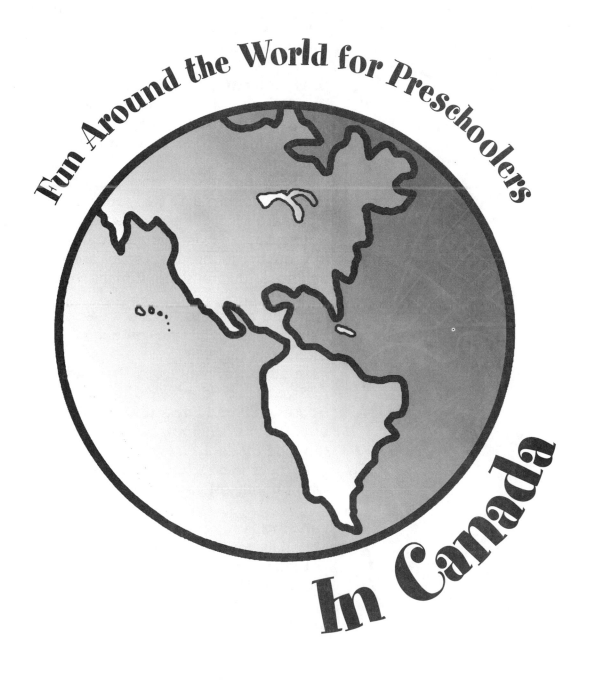

Fun Around the World for Preschoolers

In Canada

Canada

Beautiful Fall Trees
Materials: tempera paints in bright fall colors, including orange, red, and yellow; paintbrushes; newsprint or drawing paper

Give each preschooler a large sheet of newsprint or drawing paper. Encourage preschoolers to paint a fall tree. Say: September is the time when the trees in Canada turn beautiful colors. The leaves turn red, orange, and yellow.

Leaf Concentration Game
In advance, collect leaves. Be sure to gather two leaves that are similar in appearance from each tree. Mount each leaf on a small square of construction paper.

Place all squares facedown on a table. Ask preschoolers to turn over two squares to see if the two leaves are alike. Suggest preschoolers take turns continuing to turn over two leaves at a time until all matches are found. Say: Leaves are beautiful colors on Prince Edward Island, Canada, in autumn.

Painting an Island House
Materials: house pattern on page 26, paints in bright colors, paintbrushes

In advance, photocopy the house pattern.

Give each child a copy of the house pattern. Say: Houses on Prince Edward Island, Canada, are painted bright colors. The roofs are very steep so the snow can slide off easily.

Encourage preschoolers to paint their island house with brightly colored paint.

Farming Fun
Materials: toy farm equipment, toy fences, toy cattle

Lead preschoolers to build a fenced pasture for the cattle. Help them pretend to grow wheat and barley. As preschoolers play, tell them that many farmers live on Prince Edward Island, Canada.

Warm Winter Book
Materials: warm fabric scraps, scissors, heavy-duty tape

In advance, cut 3-inch squares from warm fabric scraps.

Help preschoolers choose several different fabric scraps to stack together. Tape the squares together

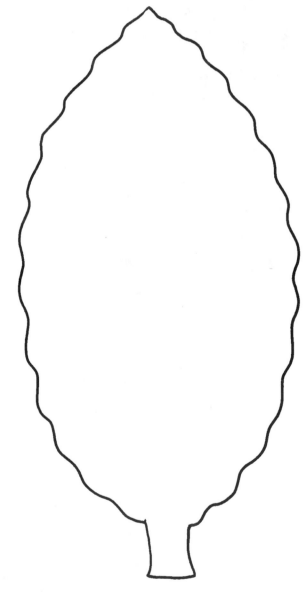

Leaf Concentration Game

to make a book. Say: Winter is very cold on Prince Edward Island. The people wear warm clothes.

Crossing the Bridge

Ask preschoolers to make two lines and join hands. Choose a volunteer to walk between the two lines as everyone sings the following words (Tune: "If You're Happy and You Know It"):

The people who come to visit cross the bridge,
the people who come to visit cross the bridge,
The people who come to visit cross the bridge to get to the Island,
The people who come to visit cross the bridge.

Explain that people who come to visit Prince Edward Island, Canada, must cross an 8-mile bridge or ride a ferryboat to get across the water.

Cleaning Potatoes

Materials: potatoes, scrub brushes, towels, plastic container, water

Invite preschoolers to help wash the potatoes and scrub the dirt away. Suggest they use the towel to dry the potatoes. Say: Many potatoes are grown on Prince Edward Island. Potatoes grow underground. That's why they are dirty.

Mitten Match

Bring a variety of pairs of winter mittens and gloves. Encourage preschoolers to help you find the ones that match to make a pair. Ask: Why are two mittens alike? (We need one mitten for each hand.).

If time permits, allow preschoolers to try on the mittens and gloves.

Farming the Soil

Materials: plastic dishpan; soil; toy, blunt-edged garden tools; gardening gloves; wheat; barley (or pictures of the grains growing)

Invite preschoolers to put on the gloves and dig in the soil with the garden tools. Show preschoolers the wheat and barley (or pictures). Say: Many farmers on Prince Edward Island, Canada, grow wheat and barley.

Potato Prints

Materials: old or sprouted potatoes, knife, disposable pie tins, liquid tempera paints, paper

Crossing the Bridge

Farming the Soil

In advance, cut potatoes in half. Cut different shapes or designs in the potato. Pour each color of paint into a separate pie tin.

Tell preschoolers that potatoes are the main product of Prince Edward Island, Canada. Demonstrate how they can dip the exposed edge of the potato (with the shape or design) in the paint and then make prints on their paper.

Ceilidhs

Materials: recording of traditional Scottish or Irish music, scarves, rhythm instruments

Explain to preschoolers that many of the people of Prince Edward Island, Canada, are of Scottish, English, and Irish heritage. Say: They love music and often gather for *ceilidhs* [KAY-lees]. These are parties featuring traditional Scottish or Irish music, dancing, songs, and stories.

Play the recording and encourage preschoolers to move to the music with their bodies as they wave the scarves. Some may want to play rhythm instruments to the music.

Ceilidhs

Painting an Island House pattern

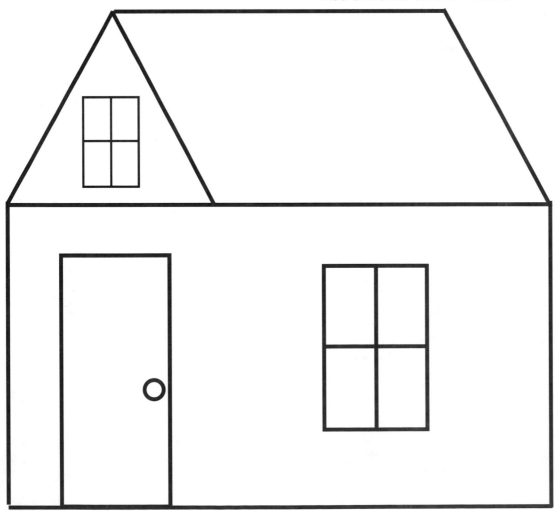

Chapter

8

Fun Around the World for Preschoolers

In China

China

Chinese Music
Check with your local library for recordings of Chinese music. Play while preschoolers are involved in their activities. Provide lengths of colorful streamers for preschoolers to hold and move to the music.

Denim Beanbags
In advance, make denim beanbags with old jeans. Cut 5-inch squares from denim, place right sides together, and sew three sides. Turn bag right side out, fill half full with beans or pebbles, and sew closed.

Invite preschoolers to move the beanbags by pushing them with their feet, by carrying them on body parts other than hands, and by balancing them on elbows or heads as they walk. Say: Boys in China like to toss beanbags with their feet.

Rice Play
Fill a dishpan with uncooked rice for the area. Provide scoops, cups, wooden spoons, and margarine tubs for preschoolers to sift and play with. Say: In China, rice is eaten every day.

Great Wall of China
Display a picture of the Great Wall of China. Working together, help preschoolers use all of the blocks and bricks to make a great wall dividing your classroom.

Chinese Meals
Materials: chopsticks; toy foods such as rice, vegetables, and egg roll; rice bowls; tea set; lace tablecloth

Invite friends to a tea party. Show how to use chopsticks to eat food. Serve pretend tea.

Winter Clothes
Place a large variety of winter clothes (hats, gloves, mittens, long underwear, coats, scarves, boots, flannel shirts) in a laundry basket. Invite preschoolers to dress up to stay warm. Talk about winter weather. Say: The winter in China is cold. People wear warm clothes.

Denim Beanbags

Great Wall of China

Catching Rice

Bring a bowl of rice and chopsticks to class. Invite preschoolers to feel and smell the rice. Show how to use the chopsticks. Give preschoolers a chance to use them, too. Say: Chinese people use chopsticks instead of forks and spoons.

Caution: This is not a tasting activity since preschoolers are handling the rice. Advise preschoolers not to lick the chopsticks or rice.

Paint Sketch Bag

Materials: self-sealing sandwich-sized bags, red and yellow paint, damp towel for leaks or clean up

In advance, prepare sketch bags by pouring a small amount of red paint in one corner and a small amount of yellow paint in the opposite corner. Seal the bags. Do not mix colors.

Show the sketch bags and let preschoolers predict what will happen if they move the paint around. Give each child a bag, and let him gently squish the colors together. Lay the bags on the table and show how to softly write with fingertips. Say: What color is your paint? People see these colors in China.

Teaching Tip: Throw out paint bags when finished.

What Comes from China?

From home and church, gather items that have labels reading Made in China on the bottom or the tag (dishes, food, toys, clothing, and so on). Print Made in China on a piece of paper and lay on the table beside these items. Show preschoolers how to look for and read the tags or stamps.

Mitten and Glove Match

Dump 12 pairs of mittens and gloves in a basket. Mix. Let a child close his eyes, choose a mitten or glove, open his eyes, and then try and find the match. Say: Winter is cold in China. People wear mittens and gloves to stay warm.

Colors of China

Materials: paper plates with *Colors of China* printed on the back; red, yellow, and orange finger paint; aprons; yarn; hole punch; scissors

After putting on aprons, let preschoolers finger paint paper plates in red, yellow, and orange. After they are dry, punch a hole at the top, make a yarn loop, and hang from the ceiling. Say: Chinese people love bright colors, like red, yellow, and orange.

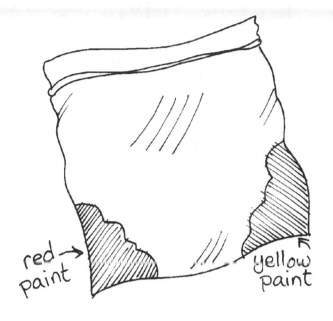

red → paint   yellow paint

mixed paint

Paint Sketch Bag

Things-That-Go-Together Book

Things-That-Go-Together Book
In advance, cut out pictures of things that match (teacup, tea bag; rice, chopsticks; hat, scarf; coat, gloves; and so on). Glue pictures on construction paper. Label pictures. Spread on a table.

Ask preschoolers to find the matching items. As they make a match, place the two pages facing each other. Staple the book along the left edge. Share.

Color Matching Game
Place one piece each of red, yellow, and orange construction paper on the floor. Gather and mix several items of each color in a pile. Invite preschoolers to sort out objects and put them on the same color of paper. Say: These are colors that Chinese people like.

Let preschoolers find more items that match.

Chapter
9

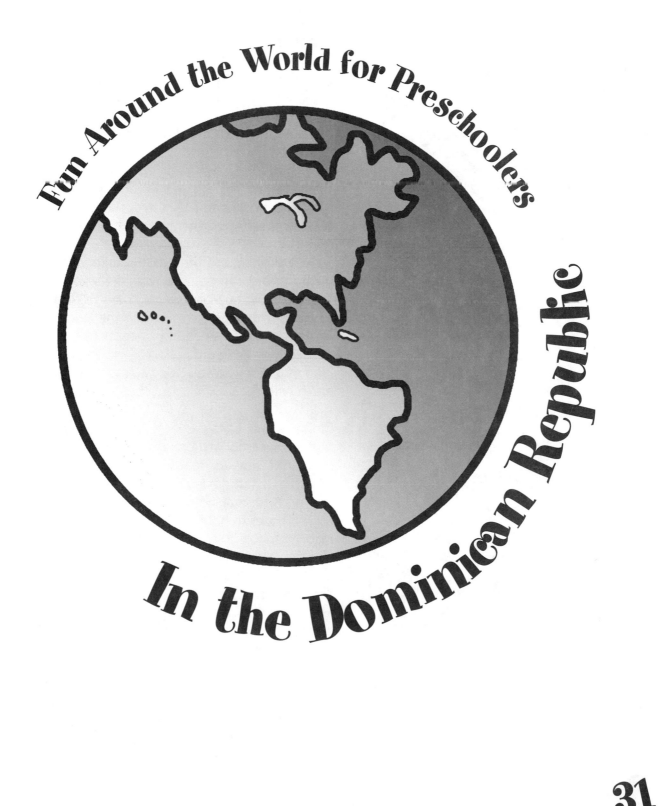

Fun Around the World for Preschoolers

In the Dominican Republic

Dominican Republic

Making Jewelry

Materials: 4 cups flour; 1 cup salt; 1½ cups water; red, yellow, blue food coloring; three containers; mixing bowl; measuring cup; measuring spoons; bright colors of yarn; plastic needles

In advance, combine flour, salt, and water to make dough. Knead for 4 or 5 minutes. Divide the dough into three containers. In each container, put 2 drops of one color of food coloring. Shape the dough into small balls then push a toothpick through the center to make a hole for stringing. Bake at 300°F for 1 hour to dry thoroughly.

Invite boys and girls to design a piece of jewelry by stringing beads on a piece of yarn. Talk about the different people who wear jewelry. Say: In the Dominican Republic, people make jewelry out of red and black coral. They sell the jewelry at the beach.

Making Jewelry

Baskets and Hats

Travel Agent

Materials: table and chairs, travel brochures and maps, pictures of the tropics, box for a computer monitor, telephone, calendar

In advance, use the box to make a computer monitor. (Another box can be used to make a keyboard.)

Invite boys and girls to role-play visiting the travel agent to plan a trip. Plan a trip to visit the Dominican Republic. Talk about what is needed in order to get their plane tickets. Ask: Do you need a passport? How long will you stay? What kind of clothes do you need? Where will you stay? How much will it cost?

Baskets and Hats

Materials: cardboard boxes, crayons and markers, fancy trim, newsprint, flowers, feathers, net, masking tape

Set up a hat-making shop. Talk about the materials and suggest ways for making hats. Decorate the boxes, and use them for hat boxes to hold the hats. Say: The people in the Dominican Republic make hats and baskets to sell. People who visit the country like to get a hat or a basket for a souvenir.

Tropical Fruit Gelatin

Materials: one package fruit-flavored gelatin, hot and cold water, canned tropical fruit, mixing bowl, spoon, paper cups, plastic spoons

Invite preschoolers to take turns putting dry gelatin in the bowl. Add hot water, keeping preschoolers away as you do. Mix thoroughly. Next ask a child to add cold water, and mix thoroughly. Ask another child to mix in the fruit. Chill until firm.

As the boys and girls are enjoying their cups of tropical fruit, talk about the different fruit that grows in the Dominican Republic.

Chapter
10

Fun Around the World for Preschoolers

In Equatorial Guinea

Thumbprint Mosquitoes

Cereal-Box Blocks

Bush Taxi

Equatorial Guinea

Thumbprint Mosquitoes
Prepare a sheet of typing paper by drawing a fire (logs, flames, smoke) in a corner. Along the bottom, print *People in Equatorial Guinea sleep by a fire at night. The smoke keeps the mosquitoes away.* Make copies. Provide a stamp pad and pencils.

Show preschoolers how to make thumbprints on the paper, away from the fire! Let them make wings, legs, and a sharp mouth on each mosquito. Read the words.

Peanut-Butter Chicken with Rice
Ingredients: 1 cup cooked, cubed chicken; cooked rice; 1 cup smooth peanut butter; 2 cups water; electric wok; spatula; spoon; paper plates; forks; posted allergy alert chart (p. 93)

After washing hands, invite preschoolers to help you place peanut butter and water in the wok. Supervise preschoolers as they help stir the sauce. After the sauce is boiling, slide the chicken into the sauce. Cook until warm. Turn off the wok.

Give each child a small scoop of rice on a paper plate. Spoon some peanut-butter chicken on top. Say: People in Equatorial Guinea grow peanuts. This is one of their favorite things to eat.
Caution: Supervise preschoolers around the wok.

Cereal-Box Blocks
Save empty cereal boxes. Loosely stuff with crumpled newspapers and tape securely closed. Help as preschoolers use the different sized boxes to build houses and towers. Say: Preschoolers in Equatorial Guinea make their own toys. These blocks are homemade.

Bush Taxi
Materials: large appliance box, two chairs, paper plates painted black, white paper plate, money

Create a bush taxi by placing the box behind the two chairs. Tape the black plates on the box for tires, and the white plate on a chair for a steering wheel. Cut off the back of the box, making a truck.

Invite preschoolers to load the bush taxi and drive to villages. Collect money before they load clothes, food, and people. Say: Sometimes, people ride in bush taxis to get to other villages. Sometimes, they have no money, so they walk.

Leaf Prints

Invite preschoolers to paint large smooth leaves with thick green paint. Show how to press the painted leaves onto cut apart paper grocery sacks. Make several prints. Say: The jungle in Equatorial Guinea has many leaves on bushes, trees, and flowers.

Thread-Spool Clackers

Place empty thread spools and long wooden blocks on the floor. Show preschoolers how to hold a spool in each hand, and tap it on the wood. Let them tap the wood, and then clack the spools together. Say: Boys and girls in Equatorial Guinea make their own toys and instruments.

Thread-Spool Clackers

Mystery Instruments

Material: plastic eggs, rocks, scrap pieces of wood, spools, blocks, sticks, masking tape, paper tubes, plastic tubs and lids

Guide preschoolers to create their own instruments. Help preschoolers problem-solve how to make their instruments work. Say: Boys and girls in Equatorial Guinea use many things to make toys and instruments. Sometimes, they use sticks or old soda cans.

Move Like Rain

Gather several pieces of blue fabric, such as scarves, dish towels, pillowcases, and fabric scraps.

Invite preschoolers to choose a piece of "water" (fabric). Holding the fabric with two hands, lead them in moving like falling rain, a rolling river, a waterfall, and a gentle stream. Lead them to show how water moves fast, slow, heavy, swirling, over rocks, and falling over a cliff. Say: Equatorial Guinea has many rivers, streams, and the nearby ocean.

Smell the Coffee

In advance, ask a parent volunteer to bring a bag of coffee beans. Place the coffee beans in a bowl. Put coffee, plastic coffee cups, and teaspoons on a table. Post the allergy alert chart (p. 93).

After washing hands, encourage preschoolers to explore the coffee. Tell preschoolers that this is a smelling, looking, and touching activity (not a tasting activity). As they put coffee beans into the cups, say: Coffee beans are grown in Equatorial Guinea.

Move Like Rain

Sponge Fun

Return coffee beans, along with a thank-you card, to your volunteer after the session.
Caution: Keep this activity away from younger preschoolers.

Sponge Fun
Materials: dry sponges, pipettes (or medicine droppers), bowl of water, towel for drying

Show preschoolers how to fill the pipettes with water and drop the water on the sponges. Watch as the sponges grow and change shapes. As sponges become saturated with water, let preschoolers wring them out over the bowl. Say: September is a part of the rainy season in Equatorial Guinea.

Chapter
11

Fun Around the World for Preschoolers

In Germany

Backpacks Are Helpful

Germany

Backpacks Are Helpful
Materials: brown paper bags, heavy string, crayons, markers, nature stickers

In advance, cut two 18-inch pieces of string for each child. Reinforce the grocery bags by turning down a 2-inch rim around the top. Punch holes on the rim. Thread the string through the holes to form loops for the arms. Around the room, place objects and pictures that relate to Germany.

Invite the boys and girls to use the markers and nature stickers to decorate their backpacks.

Talk with preschoolers about activities they enjoy doing with their families. Say: Families in Germany enjoy being together. They like to walk along the river bank. Why would a backpack be helpful on these walks?

Teaching Tip: At the end of class, suggest to the preschoolers to put their work in their backpacks.

Woodwork Shop
Materials: mat board or thick poster board; scraps of wood; glue; decorating items such as tempera paint, ribbon, scraps of paper

Encourage preschoolers to notice the texture, size, and shape of the different pieces of wood. Suggest that the mat board be used as the base to make a wood sculpture. Guide preschoolers to choose the way they want to glue the wood pieces onto the mat board. Say: Germany has many woodcraft shops. Some people study with a master wood craftsman to learn how to carve objects out of wood. Some things they learn to carve are clocks, bowls, and animals.

Teaching Tip: Invite a person who does woodwork to demonstrate woodcarving or how to cut a shape out of wood. Ask a frame shop or wood shop class to save wood scraps to use for making wood sculptures.

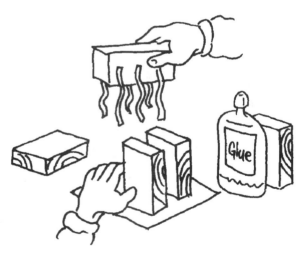

Woodwork Shop

A German Village
On a large piece of butcher paper, draw a maze of roads. Provide miniature trees and houses. Add small transportation toys. Help preschoolers set up a German village.

Decorate a Tree
Materials: small artificial tree; a plastic tub; variety of colors and sizes of ribbon, bows, garland

Secure the tree to the inside of the tub. Put the ribbon, bows, and garland in the tub. Invite the preschoolers to use the materials to decorate the tree. Say: At Christmas many people decorate an evergreen tree. The people in Germany started the custom of decorating an evergreen tree.

Decorate a Tree

The Surprise

Materials: books about dogs, a basket, a box with a lid, toy dog

Put the toy dog and the books in the box. Place the box in the area. When interest is shown in the box, give each child an opportunity to guess what is in the box. When each child has had a turn to guess, open the box to reveal the surprise. Say: Many German people have dogs for pets.

The preschoolers take turns holding the toy dog while you read a book.

Black Forest Cherry Treat

Materials: 1 can cherry pie filling; ⅛ teaspoon each cinnamon and nutmeg; 2 tablespoons melted margarine; 1 quart vanilla ice cream; clear plastic cups; plastic spoons; bowl; allergy alert chart (p. 93); poster board; pictures of ingredients in recipe

In advance, make a picture recipe card illustrating making the cherry treat. Put the recipe card and the ingredients on a table. Post the allergy chart on the door letting parents know what foods are being used.

Remind preschoolers to wash their hands. Guide them to mix the pie filling, cinnamon, nutmeg, and margarine in the bowl. Next help them spoon ice cream into the plastic cups. Lead them to pour the cherry mixture over the ice cream. Eat and enjoy. Say: Lots of forests are in Germany. The most famous one is named the Black Forest. The forest is called the Black Forest because so many of the trees are very dark green all year long.

A German Village

A Music Festival

Place several rhythm instruments in the area. Add brightly colored streamers or scarves.

Explain that the German people enjoy going to music festivals to listen to the music of their favorite musicians.

Suggest that the preschoolers plan a music festival. Talk about the rhythm instruments. Let boys and girls decide which instruments they want to play.

Black Forest Cherry Treat

Give instructions: Play your instruments loud and move fast to the music. Next play your instruments slow and soft. Move the scarves to the beat of the music.

Pick a Pair

Materials: tagboard; pictures of grapes, grape jam, apples, apple pie, hamburger, hamburger bun, hot dog, hot dog bun; two white lunch bags

In advance, mount each picture on a piece of tagboard. Laminate or cover each card with clear plastic. Put the pictures of the grapes, apples, hamburger, hot dog, in one of the bags. Put the remaining pictures in the other bag. Place the two bags in the area.

Ask preschoolers to identify the pictures. Show the matching cards from each bag. Explain that grape jam is made from grapes. The hot dog is eaten on a hot dog roll, and the hamburger is eaten on the hamburger bun.

Talk about the preschoolers' favorite foods. Say: These are some foods that people in Germany have to eat. Grapes grow on vines in a vineyard.

To play the game, four friends pick a card from one bag and four other friends pick a card from the other bag. When all the cards have been picked, each friend tries to find the friend who has the picture that relates to his picture. The preschoolers who have the matching pictures make a pair.

Pick a Pair

Chapter 12

Fun Around the World for Preschoolers

In Indonesia

Indonesia

Roof Tiles

Materials: modeling clay, plastic knives, waxed paper

Give each preschooler a mound of modeling clay on a sheet of waxed paper. Guide him to use the clay to form a roof tile. Demonstrate the shape of a tile. Say: In some parts of Indonesia the roof on a house is made of tiles. Tiles are made from clay and other natural materials God provides. The color is usually red.

Shades of Green

Materials: several shades of green crayons, drawing paper, black construction paper

Place the paper and crayons on a table. Invite preschoolers to come and draw grass. Tell them to draw in any direction and use several colors. Cut the black construction paper to make a frame for the grass drawing. Say: Many plants, trees, and grasses grow in Indonesia. Let's make green marks on our paper. This will be grass.

Caution: Be sure younger preschoolers do not place crayons in their mouths.

Colors of the Sea

Materials: small squares of scrap fabrics in shades of blue, green, and turquoise; paper plates; paste; yarn

Place a box of small fabric squares on a low table. Give each child a paper plate, and guide him to cover the paper plate with fabric so that it looks like the sea. Say: Indonesia is made up of thousands of islands. An island is land surrounded by water.

Indonesian Animals

Materials: unit blocks; toy animals such as goats, cows, chicken, dogs, cats

Guide preschoolers to make a block village. Teach these animal names with pronunciations: chicken—*ayam* [eye-yahm]; dog—*anjing* [ahn-jihng]; cat—*kucing* [koo-cheeng]; pigeon—*merpati* [mer-pah-tee].

Say: Many people in Indonesia live in small houses. They often have a goat for milking. Most families own chickens. Chickens supply eggs and meat. The city seems like the country with so many animals around.

Meet Me at the Market

Materials: empty boxes and cans, table or bookshelf, toy cash register, paper sacks or plastic bags

Shades of Green

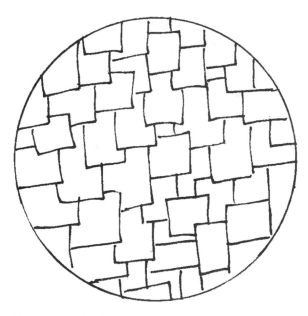

Colors of the Sea

Set up a small market. Ask for a volunteer to be the storekeeper, others will be customers. Exchange roles frequently. Say: In Indonesia women from the nearby villages walk to the market with baskets of fruit and vegetables. They sell the items to customers.

Sign Language

Note: Indonesia has schools for the Deaf. At least 2 million deaf people live in Indonesia.

Invite someone to teach preschoolers a few simple words in sign language. See deaf alphabet on page 44.

Tropical Forest Terrarium

Materials: glass gallon jar with a large opening, gravel, soil, moss, small plants, water, 2 or 3 small plastic animals

Make a tropical forest terrarium from a gallon jar. Place 1-inch of gravel in the bottom. Add 2-inches of soil. Cover with moss. Add two or three small plants and grass. Sprinkle lightly with water. Add the animals, cover the top, and place in the sunny window. Watch the moisture collect in the jar over several days. Say: Indonesia has a tropical climate. During the rainy season rain falls every day. Everything is very green.

Tropical Forest Terrarium

Sack of Grass

Materials: small cloth sack or basket of fresh cut grass; allergy alert chart (p. 93)

Post the chart. Open the basket or sack and show preschoolers the fresh cut grass. Talk about the color. Touch the grass. Ask: Do you have grass in your yard?

Say: In Indonesia women walk down the road carrying a large sack or basket of long grass on their backs. They cut the grass with a sickle. People who own goats or other animals buy the grass. The women also carry baskets of food to sell at the market.

Tasting Rice

In advance, prepare rice. Post the allergy alert chart, page 93.

Preschoolers may enjoy tasting rice. Cook the rice according to package directions, depending on the number of preschoolers present. Add a small amount of margarine and sugar. Serve warm. Say: Rice is a food eaten in Indonesia.

Tasting Rice

Tasting *Perkedel* (Potato Balls)

Tasting *Perkedel* (Potato Balls)

Materials: electric skillet; prepared, instant mashed potatoes; salt; onion flakes; egg; oil; allergy alert chart (p. 93)

Post the chart to notify parents of this activity. Prepare mashed potatoes according to package directions and the number of preschoolers present. Guide preschoolers to add seasonings and to shape the mixture into small balls. Dip in beaten egg and fry in oil. Say: Children in Indonesia enjoy eating *perkedel*. They are like our potato cakes.

Caution: Do not allow preschoolers to be near the electric skillet.

Sign Language

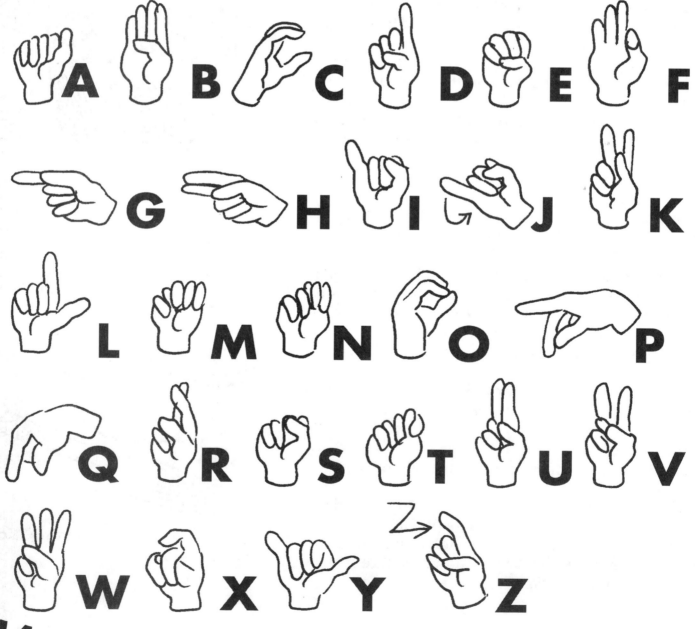

Chapter

13

Fun Around the World for Preschoolers

In Italy

Make a Pizza

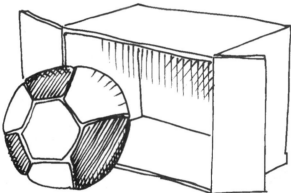

Soccer-Ball Fun

Spaghetti and Meatballs

Italy

Make a Pizza

Materials: large circles cut from manila folders (crust); the following cut from construction paper—crust-sized red circles (sauce), small reddish brown circles (pepperoni), thin green strips (peppers), small black circles (olives); yellow and white yarn cut into two-inch lengths, mixed (cheese); white glue

Suggest preschoolers make a pizza by gluing toppings on the manila-folder crust. Say: People in Italy like pizza.

Musical Art

Materials: orchestra baroque music (or any classical music), tape player, large sheets of white construction paper, watercolor paints and brushes, plastic containers of water, aprons

Place an apron on each child. Quietly play baroque music as preschoolers paint watercolor scenes. Say: Many orchestras come and play baroque music in churches and theaters.

Soccer-Ball Fun

Materials: two cardboard boxes, several soccer balls, masking tape

Make an indoor soccer field by placing a cardboard box on its side at each end of your room. Use masking tape to outline the playing field. Allow preschoolers to roll or gently tap the soccer ball towards the boxes. Say: Italians love soccer, *calcio* [CAL-choh].

Pasta Fun

Gather many examples of different shaped and colored pasta (bow tie, elbow, shells, etc.). Put several of each kind in a different self-sealing bag. Put the bags in a pasta strainer.

Lead preschoolers to compare the different sizes, colors, and shapes of the pasta. Count how many different pasta there are. Say: Italian people love to eat pasta.

Spaghetti and Meatballs

Materials: yellow and white clean foam trays cut into thin strips (pasta), red construction-paper meatballs made with a quarter sheet rolled tightly into a ball and taped together, tongs, spoons, pasta bowl, paper plates

Toss the pasta and meatballs into the pasta bowl. Let preschoolers use tongs and spoons to catch the noodles and meatballs and serve spaghetti on a plate. Say: People in Italy eats lots of pasta.

Chapter
14

Fun Around the World for Preschoolers

In Japan

Make a Kimono

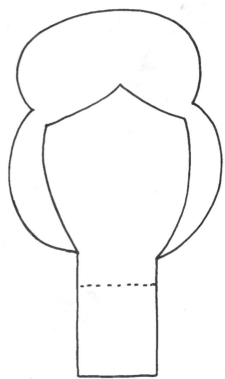

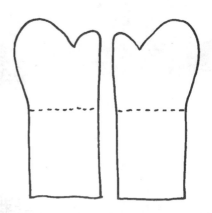

Japan

Make a Kimono

Materials: construction paper, discarded wallpaper books, markers, glue, scissors, black yarn, cutouts of Japanese doll and kimonos

In advance, enlarge and cut out the doll and kimono patterns at left for each child.

Guide preschoolers to draw a face on the doll head, then glue onto the kimono. Give preschoolers the option of drawing designs or cutting out wallpaper pieces to decorate their kimonos. The yarn can be used to make hair for the dolls.

As the preschoolers work, comment: A kimono is a long loose gown with sleeves. In Japan, the kimono is worn on special occasions. What do you think would be an occasion for people to wear the traditional Japanese kimono?

Japanese Fan

Materials: lightweight poster board, tempera paint, cotton swab, sponges, tongue depressors, stapler

In advance, cut poster board into a fan shape. Prepare several colors of tempera paint. Cut sponges into small pieces.

Guide preschoolers to paint designs on their fans. When the paint is dry, attach each fan to a tongue depressor. Say: The Japanese use a special paper called *washi* [WASH-ee] to make their fans.

Japanese Garden

Materials: a small clay saucer for each child; crayons; potting soil; spoon; small green plants; assortment of items to decorate the garden such as tiny tree branches, shells, stones; spray bottle of water

Guide a child to decorate the outside of the clay saucer with crayons then spoon potting soil to fill the container. Provide some small plants for her to plant in the soil. Suggest she choose some of the items to complete her garden.

Encourage conversation about why it is important for plants to have water and light.

Japanese Lantern

Materials: red, green, and white construction paper; scissors; stapler; crayons

Allow time for boys and girls to decorate a piece of construction paper. Guide them to lay the construction paper flat on the table. Have them fold a

1-inch strip along the two long sides. Then guide them to fold the whole sheet in half lengthwise with the two folded-up strips on the outside. Then use scissors to cut parallel rows from the centerfold up to the folded strips. Open the paper part way and roll into a cylinder on the width side. Bring the ends around until they overlap slightly and tape them together.

Big Book
Materials: five pieces of lightweight tagboard; pictures of a car, kimono, rice, chopsticks, train; hole punch; binder rings; glue

In advance, assemble the big book. Glue one picture per page. On each page, print the word in Japanese that identifies the picture. Also print the English word. Bind the book using the rings.

As a child looks at the big book, ask her to identify the pictures. Explain that the words printed under the pictures are in Japanese pronunciation and in English. Point to the Japanese word and have the child identify the picture.
car, *koo-roo-mah*; chopsticks, *hah-she*; rice, *go hahnn*; train, *den-shah*; kimono, *key-mow-noh*

Prepare a Bento Box
Materials: a shallow box for each child, foil, waxed paper, lettuce, water, bowl, cucumber, Japanese (short grain) rice, chopsticks for each child

In advance, cook the rice and slice the cucumbers. Post the allergy alert chart, page 93.

Guide preschoolers to wash their hands. Let them help wash the lettuce. Lead each child to line his box with foil. Pinch the foil to make a divider in the center of the box. Then pinch foil tightly around the edges of the box. On a piece of waxed paper, put ¼ cup of cooked rice. Then using their hands, the preschoolers shape the rice into a triangle. Next place the rice triangle in one section of the box. Add vegetables to the other section. Show preschoolers how to use the chopsticks to eat the Japanese bento. Say: Bento is a meal in a box that Japanese people often buy to eat for lunch. The bento box is divided into sections. Each section holds a different food. The people in Japan eat with chopsticks.

Japanese Lantern

Big Book

Crab Walk

Bonsai Tree

Fish Banner

Crab Walk

Help preschoolers lean backwards until their hands reach the floor. Using a musical instrument, give the signal to go. Lead them to walk backwards on all fours until they hear the signal to stop. Say: Moving like a crab is something the children in Japan like to do.

Bonsai Tree

Show preschoolers a bonsai tree. Explain that the bonsai is a miniature or small tree. Say: The Japanese people know a special way to shape the trees in small containers to keep them from growing into big trees. Many of the homes in Japan have beautiful gardens. These gardens will have one or more bonsai trees.

Whose Shoes?

Materials: bag, different sizes and styles of shoes

Put the shoes into the bag. Ask preschoolers to help you decide who would wear the shoes. Let them take turns taking a shoe out of the bag and naming whom they think would wear the shoe—the brother or the baby.

Say: In Japan it is polite to take your shoes off and put on slippers when entering a home or school.

Fish Banner

Materials: white construction paper, blue tissue paper, foil, glue, string, hole punch, black marker

In advance, cut fish shapes out of white construction paper. Cut tissue paper and foil into small pieces.

Guide preschoolers to decorate their fish shapes using the tissue and foil. With the black marker make a dot for an eye. Punch a hole near the mouth of the fish to attach string. Say: In Japan, May 5 is a special day honoring children. Parents make a banner for each boy in the family. The fish-shaped banner is hung on a pole outside the home for everyone to see how many boys are in the family.

Chapter
15

Fun Around the World for Preschoolers

In Mexico

Mexico

Mexican Maracas

Materials: paper plates, stapler and staples, tape, crayons and markers, crepe paper, dried beans

Lead preschoolers to place a handful of dried beans on a paper plate. Help them fold the plate in half, and staple securely. Put tape over the staples to protect fingers. Encourage preschoolers to draw a colorful design on the paper plate. Add crepe-paper streamers around the edge of the plate. Use instruments in music and movement activities.

Caution: Supervise carefully to ensure preschoolers do not place dried beans in their mouths.

Mexican Tissue Flowers

Materials: colored tissue paper, scissors, chenille stems

In advance, cut tissue paper into 8-by-10 pieces.

Give each child 4 to 6 squares of tissue paper in a stack. Help preschoolers fanfold the tissue paper. Tie the center of the folded tissue paper with a chenille stem. Round each end of the tissue paper. Gently pull each piece of tissue paper toward the center of the flower to make the petals. Use a chenille stem to make a leaf or add a construction-paper leaf.

A Crowded City

Materials: masking tape, toy vehicles, people figures, blocks

In advance, tape off an area of floor space in the room.

Challenge preschoolers to see how many people and buildings they can build in that limited space. Say: Mexico City is a huge city. It has more than 16 million people!

Guacamole and Chips

Materials: tortilla chips, 3 tomatoes, ½ small red onion, 2 avocados, 2 tablespoons lemon juice, 3 tablespoons cilantro (optional), 1 teaspoon salt, mixing bowl, mixing spoon, paper towels, plastic knife

In advance, post the allergy alert chart (p. 93) to notify parents of this tasting activity.

Guide preschoolers to help dice tomatoes and onions. Help a child peel the skin off the avocados and remove the seed. Put avocados in a mixing bowl, add lemon juice and salt. Suggest a child stir to mash the avocados. Then mix in the other ingredients.

Serve with tortilla chips.

Mexican Tissue Flowers

Spanish-English Colors Book

Materials: colored construction paper, scissors, glue, markers, magazines

In advance, make a colors-themed book. Each page in the book should be a different color of construction paper. On each page print the English color word and the Spanish color word.

Invite preschoolers to cut out pictures from magazines to glue to the correct page of the same color: red, *rojo* [ROH-hoh]; black, *negro* [NEH-groh]; yellow, *amarillo* [ah-mah-REE-yoh]; green, *verde* [VER-deh]; blue, *azul* [ah-ZOOL]; gray, *gris* [grees]; pink, *rosa* [ROH-sah]; white, *blanco* [BLAHN-coh]; orange, *aranjado* [ah-nah-rahn-HAH-doh]; brown, *moreno* [moh-REH-noh]; purple, *purpurado* [poor-poo-RAH-doh]. Help preschoolers pronounce the English and Spanish words. Say: People in Mexico speak English and Spanish

Spanish-English Colors Book

Market Vendor

Materials: artificial fruits. vegetables, flowers; apron

Guide preschoolers to pretend they are street vendors at a local market in Mexico. Say: Many people buy their fruits, vegetables, and flowers at the local markets throughout Mexico.

Greetings

Lead preschoolers to practice greeting one another as if they were in Mexico. Teach them to say: *buenos días* [BWAY-nohs DEE-ahs] (good morning) and *adiós* [ah-dee-OHS] (good-bye).

Explain that women greet each other with a kiss. This is true for a woman and man exchanging greetings as well. A man greeting a man extends a handshake and hug.

Avocado Pit

Prepare an avocado pit as directed and invite preschoolers to observe its growth each week. Wash the avocado pit under cool running water and gently wipe away and remove any of the green fruit that might be on the pit. Rinse it well and then blot dry with a paper towel. Carefully push three toothpicks into the pit about a half-inch deep. The toothpicks will help suspend the avocado pit to keep the top part of the pit in fresh air and the fat base of the pit under the surface of the water. Suspend the pit over a jar filled with water. The toothpicks will rest on the rim of the jar and hold the pit in place so it doesn't

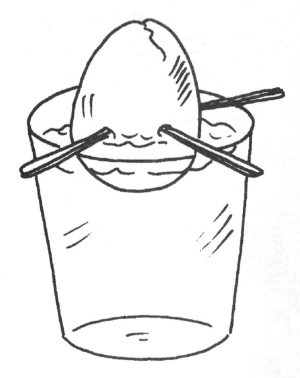

Avocado Pit

Feeling Box

sink to the bottom. Always check the water level in the jar to see that the water is covering the base of the pit by about an inch. Place the glass in a bright windowsill. In a few weeks, the top of the pit will split and a stem sprout will emerge from the top and roots will begin to grow at the base.

Say: People in Mexico like to eat avocados.

Feeling Box
Cut a hole large enough for preschoolers' hands to fit through in the lid of a shoe box. Place small items that you'd see in Mexico in the box, and ask preschoolers to reach into the box. Guide them to describe how the object feels and to guess what it might be. After each preschooler has touched the object, take the object out and reveal what was in the box. Continue as long as preschoolers show interest.

Pounding Corn

Pounding Corn
Materials: ears of dried corn, corn tortillas, two large flat stones, two fist-sized round stones

Invite preschoolers to shell the corn, and grind it on the flat stones with the round stones. Show them the corn tortillas. Say: Tortillas are one of the foods eaten in Mexico. They are made from corn.

Chapter
16

Fun Around the World for Preschoolers

In Poland

Oatmeal-Container Book

Wading-Pool Book

Guitars and Scarves

Poland

Oatmeal-Container Book
Cover an empty oatmeal container with construction paper. In random order, print each preschooler's name two times on the paper. Put bright stickers around the container. Ask preschoolers to find both of their names. As they read the names, say: People in Poland have a special holiday for names, called a name day. Each person has a day during the year on which all the people with the same name celebrate.

A Polish Household
Materials: clean stuffed dogs, leashes, dresses, jeans, shirts, food, toy utensils, table, chairs, kitchen

Pretend to be a family in Poland. Let preschoolers select a pet dog, and attach a leash to it. Help preschoolers dress-up in dresses or jeans. Decide who will cook meals, and who will walk the dog. Say: Families in Poland dress like we do. Many families have pet dogs. Sometimes, a grandma or grandpa lives with families.

Wading-Pool Book
Materials: small wading pool; construction paper; picture of a Bible (*Biblia* [bib-LEE-ah]), a mother (*mama* [MAH-mah]), a father (*tata* [TAH-tah]), a dog (*pies* [PEE-es]), and a cat (*kot* [kaht]); glue; marker; tape

Place each picture on a piece of construction paper. Write the name beneath each picture, in English and Polish. Tape the pictures in the wading pool. Invite preschoolers to sit in the pool and read the pictures. Help them pronounce Polish words. Say: People in Poland speak Polish.

Guitars and Scarves
Play a CD of instrumental guitar music. Give each preschooler a chiffon scarf. Invite them to move the scarves to the music. Provide a toy guitar and lead them to play along to the music. Say: Music is important to people in Poland.

Classical Music
Play classical music quietly in the background. As preschoolers notice the music, show pictures of orchestras. Say: Many artists, musicians, and writers have come from Poland.

If available, show a piece of music written by Frederic Chopin. Point to the notes in the piece, and say: Frederick Chopin wrote this music. He was a famous composer born in Poland.

Chapter 18

Fun Around the World for Preschoolers

In Scotland

Scotland

Woolly Sheep and Lambs

Materials: sheep and lamb pattern at left, scissors, cotton balls, glue, wiggly eyes (check craft stores), construction paper, crayons or markers

In advance, trace the patterns onto construction paper for each child to have one.

Help preschoolers cut out the sheep and lamb from the construction paper. Guide preschoolers to glue cotton balls onto their animals. Lead them to glue a wiggly eye to each animal. Suggest preschoolers glue their sheep and lamb to a piece of construction paper. Encourage them to add details such as mountains, grass, and fences using crayons or markers.

Say: Many sheep and lambs are in Scotland. Their wool is used to make hats, scarves, and mittens.

Castles and Cathedrals

Encourage preschoolers to build castles and cathedrals with the blocks. Say: Many beautiful old castles and cathedrals are in Scotland. A cathedral is a very large church building.

Suggest preschoolers use people figures and toy vehicles to pretend that people are walking and driving to the castles and cathedrals.

Sports Spectacular

Invite interested preschoolers to gently roll or kick a soccer ball back and forth to each other. Say: The Scottish people play soccer, but they call it football.

Sheep, Cattle, and Pigs

Materials: toy sheep, cattle, and pigs; plastic fences; farm toys and props (tractor, farmer figure, etc.)

Guide preschoolers to pretend they are farmers who raise sheep, cattle, and pigs. Say: Many of the Scottish people raise animals. People visiting Scotland often see sheep and cattle grazing on the green mountains.

Scots Tablet

Materials: 4 cups granulated sugar; ½ cup (1 stick) butter; ½ cup water; ½ cup milk; large can sweetened condensed milk; 1 teaspoon vanilla extract; hot plate; saucepan; mixing spoon; buttered dish or pan; allergy alert chart (p. 93)

Woolly Sheep and Lambs

Guide preschoolers to help you make this Scottish treat. Put the sugar, butter, water, and milk into a large, heavy pan over a low heat and stir until the sugar is completely dissolved. Bring to a boil and boil for 10 minutes without stirring. Stir in the condensed milk, and boil for 10 more minutes. Remove from the heat and add vanilla extract. Beat the mixture for 1 minute and pour into a buttered, shallow dish. Cool and cut into squares.

Tartan-Plaid Paintings

Materials: white construction paper, tempera paints, paintbrushes or rollers, plaid clothing articles or plaid fabrics

Show the fabric to preschoolers. Say: Scotland is known for plaid fabrics. The men sometimes wear a special piece of clothing called a kilt that is made from plaid fabric. You can make your own plaid pattern.

Help preschoolers paint straight horizontal lines across their pieces of paper with one color of paint. Turn the paper and help preschoolers paint lines of a contrasting color across the first lines.

Tartan-Plaid Paintings

Suppertime

Materials: cookies; decaffeinated, lukewarm tea; plates; cups; napkins; allergy alert chart (p. 93)

Post the allergy alert chart to notify parents of this activity. Explain to preschoolers that the Scottish people have a bedtime snack they call supper. It usually includes biscuits (cookies) and hot tea. Sometimes toast and jam are served. Serve the preschoolers a biscuit and a cup of tea. As they enjoy supper, talk about some of the different names for food in Scotland (mashed potatoes, *tatties*; potato chips, *crisps*; candies, *sweeties*).

Caution: Be sure that the tea is not too hot for preschoolers to drink.

Suppertime

Barefoot Run

Invite preschoolers to take off their shoes and socks. Have them place their socks inside their shoes. Stack all the shoes into a pile. Divide the preschoolers into two teams. Explain that the first person on each team will run to the stack and find her socks and shoes and put them on. Then they will return to the back of the line and the next person on the team will run to the pile and do the same. This will continue until one team has finished. Say: The Scottish people have beautiful green yards, which they call gardens, and hills. They like to run barefoot in the grass.

Scottish Ceilidh

Materials: audio recording of Scottish folk music, drums and/or rhythm instruments

Explain that people in Scotland enjoy *ceilidh* [KAY-lee] dancing. This is dancing to Scottish folk music, often with live accordion, guitar, violin, and drums. Play the audio recording, and invite preschoolers to move to the music and/or play the instruments.

Teaching Tip: Invite a musician who plays the accordion, guitar, violin, or drums to visit the class and demonstrate how the instrument is played.

Scottish Scents

Materials: small film canisters and lids, coffee, tea, raisins, jam, blindfold or piece of fabric

In advance, fill each film canister with a small amount of one of the food items.

Say: The Scots like to eat many of the same foods we do. Each one of these containers has something in it. Let's play a game and see if you can guess what is in each one.

Ask for a volunteer to be blindfolded. Let the volunteer smell the contents of the container and guess what it might be. Continue until all the containers have been opened. Allow preschoolers to look in each container after all have been opened.

Explain that the Scots like to drink coffee and hot tea. They put raisins in their scones, similar to our biscuits. They eat jam on their toast for supper, which is a bedtime snack.

Rivers and Lakes

Materials: large plastic tub; water toys (funnels, pitchers, cups, boats); towel

Fill the tub with water. Place the toys nearby. As preschoolers show interest, encourage them to play in the water with the water toys. Say: Scotland has many lakes and rivers. Scotland is also near the Atlantic Ocean.

Help preschoolers dry their hands on the towel as they finish playing.

Scottish Scents

Rivers and Lakes

Chapter 19

Fun Around the World for Preschoolers

In South Korea

South Korea

Spring Blossoms

Materials: easel, large newsprint, tempera paints in bright pastel and spring colors, smocks

In advance, cut large blossoms from the newsprint and place on the easel.

Invite preschoolers to put on a smock and paint a spring blossom using the pastel and spring colors of paint you have provided. Say: Many beautiful flowers bloom in South Korea in the spring.

Watercolor Paintings

Materials: white paper, watercolor paints, paintbrushes, small cups of water

Allow preschoolers to use the watercolors to paint a picture. Encourage them to blend the colors or use less water to make a more vibrant hue. Say: Many beautiful paintings are in South Korea. You can paint, too!

Teaching Tip: Demonstrate how to use the water to rinse the paintbrush before changing colors.

Spring Blossoms

Colorful Ceramics and Pottery

Materials: air-dry clay, bright blue and white tempera paints

Lead preschoolers to create a simple bowl or vase from the clay. Allow time for the clay to dry. Lead preschoolers to paint the clay white. Encourage them to decorate the white container with bright blue designs. Say: Many pieces of beautiful pottery are made in South Korea. The artists use their hands to make beautiful ceramics from clay.

A Big City with Many Families

Materials: blocks of all sizes and shapes, people figures, toy vehicles, area carpet with roadways

Encourage preschoolers to build a large city where many people live. As preschoolers play, say: South Korea has many large cities with lots of people living in them.

Visit in a Korean Home

Materials: variety of stuffed fancy pillows, low table, chopsticks

As preschoolers enter the room, welcome them to your Korean home and help them remove their shoes. Explain that in Korea, children bow to their

Colorful Ceramics and Pottery

elders. Lead preschoolers to sit on the fancy pillows around the low table and pretend to eat a meal together. Say: The Korean people remove their shoes and put on slippers when entering a house. They eat at a low table while sitting on fancy pillows.

Tunnels and Vehicles
Materials: a variety of toy vehicles, empty shoe boxes, scissors, blocks

In advance, cut an opening on each end of the shoe boxes to make a tunnel.

Lead preschoolers to pretend to drive the toy vehicles through the tunnels and over elevated highways (made from blocks), hills, and mountains. Say: South Korea has many hills and mountains. Sometimes the people drive through tunnels or on a highway bridge over valleys

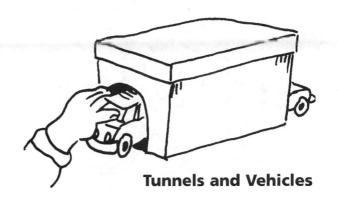

Tunnels and Vehicles

Korean Paper Fan
Materials: white drawing paper, crayons or markers, transparent tape

Ask preschoolers to draw pictures of things for which they are thankful on both sides of a piece of drawing paper. Help preschoolers accordion-fold the paper. Pinch the pleated paper in the center. Bring up the two sides and tape together to make a fan. Encourage preschoolers to fan themselves or a friend as they listen to the music again.

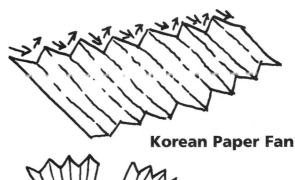

Korean Paper Fan

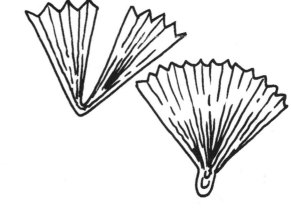

Honk! Honk!
Explain that South Korean cities have many loud noises, including honking buses and car horns. Show preschoolers a bicycle horn. Direct them to walk around the room and pretend to be cars. Tell preschoolers to listen for the honk of the horn. Say: If I honk the horn two times, get two people in your group. If I honk the horn three times, get three people in your group.

Continue to play until preschoolers lose interest.

Matching Fish Game
Materials: wallpaper sample books, scissors, fish pattern

In advance, copy and cut the simple fish pattern on page 64 to trace onto wallpaper samples. Cut two fish from each wallpaper pattern.

Place the fish facedown on a table or carpeted area. Lead preschoolers to take turns turning over

Matching Fish Game

two fish at a time. If the fish match, the child keeps the match and takes another turn. If the fish do not match, the next preschooler takes his turn. Continue until all matching pairs of fish have been found. Say: Many people are fishermen in South Korea.

Matching Shoes Game
Direct preschoolers to remove their shoes and place them in a large stack. Lead preschoolers in a game to locate their own shoes and put them back on their feet. Say: In South Korea, people usually take their shoes off when they enter a house. They remove their shoes and put on slippers.

Matching Shoes Game

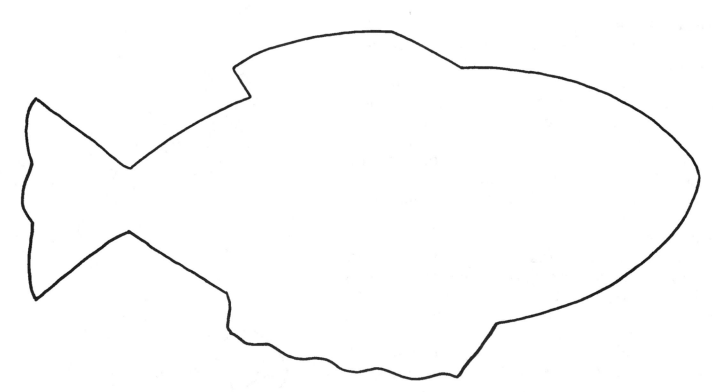

Matching Fish Game Pattern

Chapter
20

Fun Around the World for Preschoolers

In Tanzania

Tanzania

Little Kangas
Materials: 16-inch square pieces of muslin (edges zigzagged), acrylic craft paints, brushes, aprons

Invite preschoolers to make bold designs on a *kanga* [KAHN-gah] with markers and paints. Say: Women in Tanzania wear *kangas*. A *kanga* is a large, brightly colored piece of fabric.

Tropical Flowers
Materials: bright colored tissue paper (each sheet cut into four pieces), scissors, green chenille stems, curling ribbon

Show how to fold each piece of tissue paper in half lengthwise. Along the fold, cut fringe, leaving 1 inch of paper uncut. Roll the paper into a tube, twist the bottom, and wrap a chenille stem around the flower base. Hold the flower upright and lightly smash down the petals. Help preschoolers tie pieces of curling ribbon to the flower base. Say: Beautiful flowers bloom during the rainy season in Tanzania.

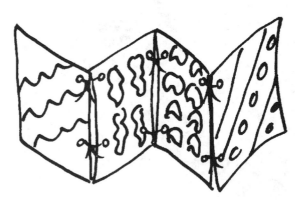

Tropical Flowers

Game Park
Display a picture of a game park. Help preschoolers use wooden blocks to make an outline of a game reserve. Give preschoolers toy safari animals, 4-wheel drive vehicles, and people. Say: Tanzania has several wild game parks. Tourists enjoy seeing the animals.
Teaching Tip: Check local toy stores or catalogs for sets of African animals.

Fabric Book
Materials: 10-inch square cardboard pieces, hot glue gun, African print fabric cut into 11-inch squares, awl, yarn, scissors

Prepare this book by gluing a piece of fabric on each side of a piece of cardboard, overlapping the edges to cover the sides. Punch two holes on opposite sides of each page, and loosely tie with pieces of yarn. Display the fabric book by standing it up accordion-style on the floor. Show to babies and toddlers.

Fabric Book

Kanga Skirts
Add colorful 1-yard pieces of fabric and several baby dolls to the area. Demonstrate how to wear

kangas by tying fabric around the waist for a skirt, and adding another for a wrap. Let preschoolers experiment by carrying a doll tied onto their backs with another piece of fabric.

Teaching Tip: Allow boys to try on *kangas* and carry the babies too.

Drums

Materials: an empty oatmeal canister covered with white construction paper for each child, markers, 1-inch wide ribbon, awl, scissors

In advance, punch two holes in the top of oatmeal canisters and attach a piece of ribbon, making a carrying loop.

Invite preschoolers to draw African designs on the drum covering. Show how to wear the ribbon around the neck, and play the drum by tapping fingertips on the lid. Say: At night, some people in Tanzania play drums.

Drums

Jump the River

Spread a blue sheet along the floor to resemble a river. Encourage preschoolers to jump the river, pretend to wade in the river, or make a bridge. As preschoolers jump, wade, or make the bridge, sing to the tune of "Here We Go 'Round the Mulberry Bush":

This is the way we jump the river.
Jump the river.
Jump the river.
This is the way we jump the river.
The river in Tanzania.
Continue with *wade in the river.*

Coconut Tasting

Materials: fresh coconut; hammer; nail; cutting board; bowl; grater; cups; allergy alert chart (p. 93)

In advance, post the chart, and wash hands.

Place the coconut on the cutting board, and make a hole in the top with the nail and hammer. Pour the coconut milk into a bowl. Let volunteers try and break the coconut with a hammer. After the coconut is broken, peel off the shell, and grate the coconut pieces. Taste. Say: In Tanzania, many foods are cooked with coconut.

Caution: Carefully supervise hammering.

Jump the River

Mortar and Pestle

Sisal Stuff
Place a sisal floor rug (rough, outdoor rug) and a piece of sisal rope on a table. Invite preschoolers to touch and smell the sisal. Say: Sisal is from a plant. Tanzania grows a lot of sisal.

Mortar and Pestle
Post the allergy alert chart (p. 93). Place a mortar, pestle, and a bowl of popcorn kernels on a table. Guide preschoolers to grind the corn into corn flour. Talk about how long it takes. Say: Corn is a favorite food in Tanzania. Corn is eaten every day.

Chapter
21

Fun Around the World for Preschoolers

In Thailand

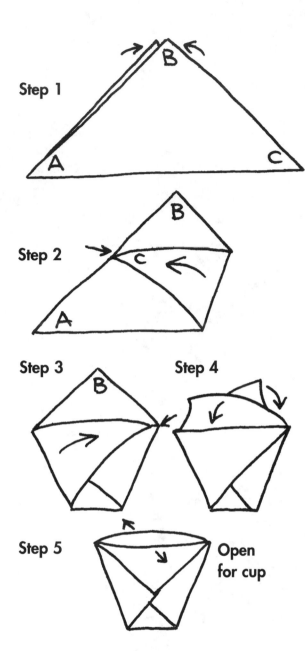

Step 1

Step 2

Step 3

Step 4

Step 5

Open for cup

Origami Paper Cups

Thailand

Origami Paper Cups

Say: Origami is the art of paper folding. The people of Thailand not only use paper, but also banana leaves!

Since banana leaves are in short supply in the United States, use paper for this fun project. These are not only pretty, but functional. They actually hold water.

Step 1

Fold an 8½-by-8½ square of paper in half diagonally, with resulting triangle point at the top.

Step 2

Take corner C and fold to center point between A and B.

Step 3

Take corner A and fold to center point between B and C.

Step 4

Fold down the front flap of corner B to the front of the cup and the back flap of corner B to the back.

Step 5

Press in top corners of cup to open—then enjoy!

Blot Pictures

Materials: white construction paper, liquid food coloring, glue

Lead preschoolers to fold their construction paper in half lengthwise, then open it back up. Instruct preschoolers to drizzle glue on one half of the paper, then drop two drops of each color food coloring onto the glue. Refold the paper and rub very gently to flatten. Unfold the paper again, and allow for drying.

Say: These designs look much like the designs on the fabric Thai women make on their looms.

Elephants

From your local library, check out books with realistic pictures of elephants.

Place the books in the area and read to an interested preschooler. Encourage conversation about elephants. Say: People see elephants every day in Thailand.

Thai Dessert

Post the allergy alert chart, page 93, on the door to inform parents of this tasting activity.

Bananas in Coconut Milk

2 cups coconut milk (available in cans or as powder in imported food section of supermarket)
2 tablespoons brown sugar
½ cup granulated sugar
¼ teaspoon salt
4 bananas

In advance, combine the first four ingredients in a saucepan and bring to a boil. Remove from heat.

Peel bananas. Give preschoolers plastic knives and allow them to help you slice the bananas in the coconut milk mixture. (This dessert can be eaten warm or cold.)

Panungs

Provide large pieces of colorful fabric for preschoolers to use as *panungs*. As preschoolers dress up, say: In Thailand villages, the men wear their *panungs* wrapped around their waists to above their ankles. The women wear theirs wrapped above their chests to above their ankles. Thai people also remove their shoes before entering a house.

Panungs

Marketplace

Materials: baskets or small bags for each child; plastic fruit; small boxes of dry food stuffs and cans or toy food; other items, such as play jewelry, bowls, utensils, etc.

In advance, set up the room to resemble a small market. Have a place for the fruit, a place for dry goods, etc.

As preschoolers arrive, give each one a basket and encourage him to "shop" in the market. Give preschoolers time to shop, and then let them spread out what they bought on the table. Say: Some Thai people shop in outdoor markets every day.

Flower Arranging

Provide a vase and real or artificial flowers for preschoolers to arrange. Say: In Thailand a lot of rain falls, so plants grow very well. Many beautiful flowers grow in Thailand.

Caution: If using real flowers, post the allergy alert chart on page 93 to notify parents of this activity.

Marketplace

Takraw

Say: To play *takraw* in Thailand, a woven wicker ball is sent back and forth over a net or string stretched between two points, using no hands. Elbows, knees, feet, heads are OK, just no hands.

Provide a soft foam ball and a net or string for preschoolers to play *takraw*.

What's in the Sock?

Place familiar objects related to Thailand one at a time in a tube sock, such as a banana, toy elephant, flower, colorful fabric, etc. Ask a preschooler to feel the object and tell what it is. If necessary, give helpful hints so he will be successful. Say: This is something you can eat. It is yellow.

Flower Water Globe

Lead younger preschoolers to smell a flower. Then place the flower in a plastic jar filled with water. Screw the lid on tightly. Encourage preschoolers to roll and shake the jar. Say: I see a flower in this jar. Many pretty flowers grow in Thailand.

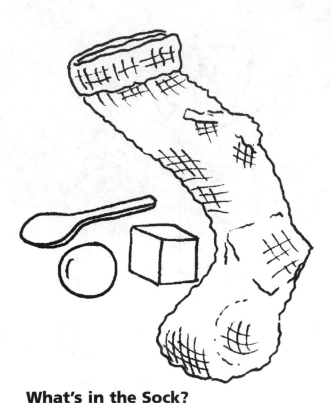

What's in the Sock?

Chapter 22

Fun Around the World for Preschoolers

In Togo

Togo

Head Scarves

Materials: 18-inch squares of muslin, sewing machine, acrylic craft paints, paper plates, brushes, aprons

In advance, sew small hems on muslin squares. Squirt small amounts of paint on several plates.

Invite preschoolers to don an apron and paint designs on a head scarf. Say: Many women in Togo wear head scarves.

Head Scarves

Scarves and Blocks

Gather wooden blocks, and an opaque, a sheer, and a solid scarf. Hide a block under each scarf on the floor. Let younger preschoolers discover what is under the scarves. Place a scarf over your face. If a baby enjoys the game, place a scarf over her face.

Caution: Supervise scarves being over faces.

Rope Painting

Materials: 6-inch pieces of rope, tempera paint in pie pans, large construction paper, aprons

After preschoolers put on aprons, let them experiment with rope and paint. Show how to dip the rope in paint and make a rope print on the paper. Say: Girls in Togo like to jump rope.

Rope Painting

Balloon Rattle

In advance, make balloon rattles with small helium-quality balloons and birdseed. Pour ½ teaspoon birdseed into each balloon, inflate to about tennis-ball size, and tie each one closed. Place in a smooth container.

Invite preschoolers to play the rattles by shaking, tapping, and gently tossing the balloons, below eye level. Say: Togolese people enjoy gourds that make rattle sounds.

Caution: Immediately throw away broken balloons and birdseed as they are choking hazards.

Scarves and Baskets

Place a variety of scarves and flat-bottomed baskets on a table. Invite preschoolers to move while balancing the scarves and baskets on their heads. Add plastic fruit or foods to the baskets. Say: Women and children in Togo carry things on their heads.

Notebooks and Pens

Provide notebooks and pens for preschoolers. As they draw and print on the pages, say: Most boys and girls in Togo do not have school supplies. Many do not go to school because their parents cannot afford the uniforms, school fee, and school supplies.

Play-Dough Huts

Make brown play dough (p. 76). Give preschoolers play dough and some straw. Look at pictures of huts as they build round huts and place straw roofs on top. Say: Many people in Togo live in mud huts. The roofs are made of straw.

Jump Ropes

Place three 6-foot pieces of rope on the floor. Encourage preschoolers to jump over them. Have two preschoolers hold a rope a short distance above the ground or swing it back and forth while their friends jump over the top. Say: Girls in Togo like jump ropes.

Caution: Supervise carefully when using ropes around young preschoolers.

Sleeping Mattress

Materials: construction paper, hole punch, 44-inch pieces of yarn with masking tape on one end to form a needle, shredded newspaper

Prepare the paper by stapling two sheets together at the corners. Punch holes 2 inches apart around the outside edge. Tie yarn to a corner hole.

Make a stuffed mattress. Show how to sew three sides, stuff with newspaper, and then sew the fourth side. Feel the mattress. Say: In Togo, men gather elephant grass and use it to stuff mattresses.

What Is a Gourd?

Purchase several different gourds. Place in a basket. Invite Katie to look at and touch the gourds. Ask her to shake the gourds and listen for sounds. Say: Togolese people use dried gourds for instruments.

Woven Baskets

Display a variety of baskets on a colorful blanket. Invite preschoolers to examine and compare the baskets. Say: People in Togo often use baskets.

Note: Shop at thrift stores or borrow baskets from friends.

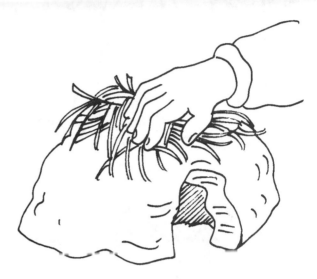

Play-Dough Huts

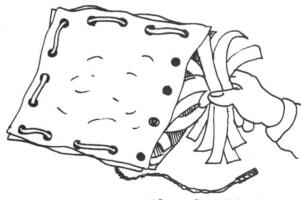

Sleeping Mattress

Hula-Hoop Scarf Game

Suspend several hula-hoops from the ceiling. Provide preschoolers with brightly colored scarves. Let them try and toss the scarves through the hoops. Count how many "baskets" they make. Say: People in Togo wear bright colors.

Hula-Hoop Scarf Game

Play Dough Recipe

3 cups flour
1 cup salt
1 tablespoon alum
2 tablespoons oil
food coloring
3 cups boiling water

Mix together all ingredients except water and coloring.
Put food coloring in measuring cup, and add water to it.
Pour water in with other ingredients.
Mix and knead well.
Store in a covered container until ready to use.

Chapter
23

Fun Around the World for Preschoolers

In Uruguay

Uruguay

Design a T-Shirt

Materials: T-shirts, white paper, fabric crayons, newspaper, iron

Guide preschoolers to use the fabric crayons to draw a design on a piece of white paper. Remind them to make heavy marks on the paper so that when the design is transferred to the T-shirt, it will show the bright colors.

Place the T-shirt on a pad of newspaper. Demonstrate how to place the design facedown on the shirt. Press with a warm iron, using a firm straight-down pressing motion, transferring the design onto the shirt. Say: The children in Uruguay like to play soccer and other sports. The players wear a special T-shirt that has the name of their team.

Caution: An adult needs to do the ironing or supervise older preschoolers as they iron.

Design a T-Shirt

Mini Wheat Pizzas

Home on the Ranch

Materials: toy cows and horses, logs to make fences, bandanas, hats and boots, picture of a *gaucho*

Explain that in Uruguay the men who take care of cattle are ranch hands called *gauchos* [GOW-chohs]. Say: The country of Uruguay has lots of grazing land for cattle. The *gauchos* have a very important job. To help them do their job they wear a special outfit.

As preschoolers play with the items, show the picture of the *gaucho*. Identify the parts of his outfit.

Mini Wheat Pizzas

Materials: wheat crackers; pizza sauce; grated mozzarella cheese; spoon; baking sheet; paper plates; allergy alert chart (p. 93)

Remind preschoolers to wash their hands. Provide two or three wheat crackers for each child. To make mini pizzas, guide each child to spread pizza sauce on each cracker, then sprinkle grated mozzarella cheese on top. Heat the pizzas in an oven or microwave until cheese melts. Say: The crackers are made from wheat. Wheat is a grain. Wheat is grown in Uruguay. Can you name other foods that are made from wheat?

Teaching Tip: Display examples of these grains: wheat, corn, rice, oats.

Blow Wind Blow

Materials: three different colors of tempera paint, paper, spoons, three plastic bowls, box lid

In advance, put a different color of tempera paint in each of the three bowls. Place a spoon in each bowl.

Lay a piece of paper in the box lid. Guide preschoolers to drop spoonfuls of paint onto the paper. Ask them to watch what happens when they gently blow. Engage the preschoolers to talk about how the wind sometimes blows gently and sometimes blows hard. Explain that Uruguay has a lot of flat land and not many mountains. Very quickly the weather can change, often causing a windstorm.

Which Comes First?

Materials: corn kernels, cornmeal, corn bread muffins, wheat, bag of flour, loaf of bread, grains of rice, box of rice, rice cakes or rice cereal, poster board, markers

In advance, divide the poster board into three columns. On the first column, draw an ear of corn and print the word *corn*. In the second column, draw a picture of wheat growing in the field and print the word *wheat*. For the last column draw a rice paddy and print the word *rice*.

Show the three grains to the preschoolers. Say: These are grains used to make different foods. These grains grow in many places. One place where they grow is Uruguay. Let's name some foods made from each of these grains.

Encourage conversation about the sequence from the grain to the finished product. Under each grain on the chart, invite a child to put in sequence getting grain from the field to the baked food item.

Play Ball

Materials: blocks; pictures of a baseball, bat, glove; toy people figures; four carpet squares

Guide preschoolers to use the carpet squares for bases as set up at a baseball diamond. Encourage conversation about the rules used in playing baseball. Suggest using the other props to play a game of baseball.

Roll and Tell

Provide a cardboard or plastic cube. On each side of the cube, draw or glue a picture that relates to Uruguay.

Blow Wind Blow

Which Comes First?

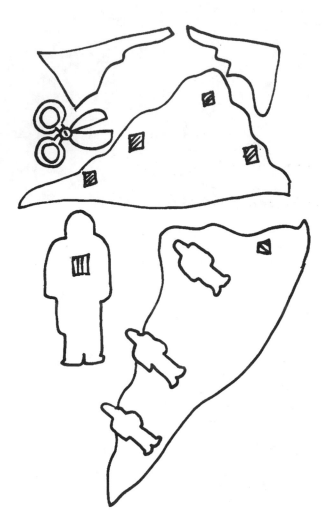

Mountain Climbing

Invite a child to roll the cube. When the cube stops rolling, ask her to tell about the picture on the side of the cube facing her.

Guess What?

Materials: four small bags, baseball, seashell, jump rope, toy cow

Place one object in each bag. Fold each bag down to prevent the preschoolers seeing the contents. Describe how to play the game. Say: I'll pass one of the bags around. You are to use your ears and not your eyes to find out what is in the bag. Listen to the clue I will give you to help you guess what's in the bag.

Give clues until the object in each bag has been identified.

Mountain Climbing

Materials: brown paper, scissors, marker, masking tape, pictures of people, hook-and-loop fastener

In advance, cut the shape of a mountain out of the brown paper. Attach pieces of fastener at different locations going up different sides of the mountain. Cut out the people pictures. Put the opposite fastener side on the back of each picture. Print *Sugar Loaf Mountain* on the paper and tape to a wall.

Tell the boys and girls that boys and girls in Uruguay enjoy climbing Sugar Loaf Mountain. Suggest they use the people figures to climb the mountain.

Chapter
24

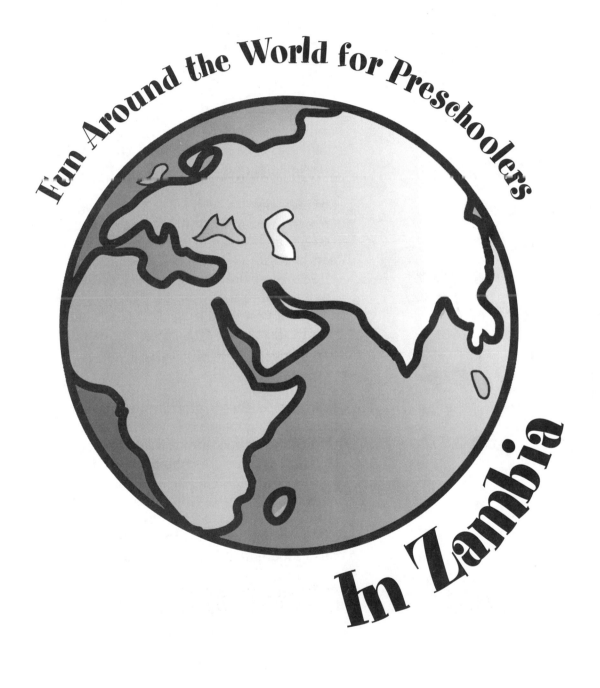

Fun Around the World for Preschoolers

In Zambia

Zambia

Weaving Mats

In advance, for each preschooler, fold a large sheet of construction paper (12-by-18 inches) in half, widthwise. Starting on the folded edge, cut lines 1½ inches apart, stopping 1½ inch from the open edge. Unfold the resulting loom, then cut 1½-inch strips from another sheet of construction paper.

Guide preschoolers to take the strips and "weave" over and under the strips in the loom. Tape the ends of the strips to the loom. As they work, say: The Lozi people in Zambia are basket weavers.

Making Toys

Provide chenille craft stems, thread spools, potato-chip cans, or film canisters for the area. Guide preschoolers to create their own toys. Say: In Zambia, children make toys.

Praise the preschoolers for their efforts.

Lozi Snacks

Provide some or all of the following for preschoolers to taste; roasted peanuts, sugarcane, mangoes, guavas, roasted ears of corn.

Say: These are some of the foods the Lozi people of Zambia like to eat as snacks.

Caution: Post the allergy alert chart, page 93, to notify parents of this tasting activity. Also remember do not give peanuts to younger preschoolers.

Lozi Village

In advance, check with furniture and appliance stores for large washing machine/dryer boxes or refrigerator boxes. Cut off top flaps, then turn upside down and cut a doorway large enough for preschoolers to go through.

Place boxes in the area and provide area rugs, towels, or mats for preschoolers to place inside. Provide small sticks of wood for preschoolers to make a pretend fire in the center of the village. Say: The Lozi village people in Zambia live in small square mud huts, and do their cooking outside.

Chitenges

Lozi women in Zambia wear a long, rectangular shaped piece of cloth called a *chitenge* [chih-TENG-eh] wrapped around their skirts or dresses. Women who have babies always carry a second *chitenge* with them to carry their babies on their backs.

Provide colorful beach towels for preschoolers to use as *chitenges*. Place dolls in the area and guide preschoolers to use *chitenges* to carry the dolls on their backs.

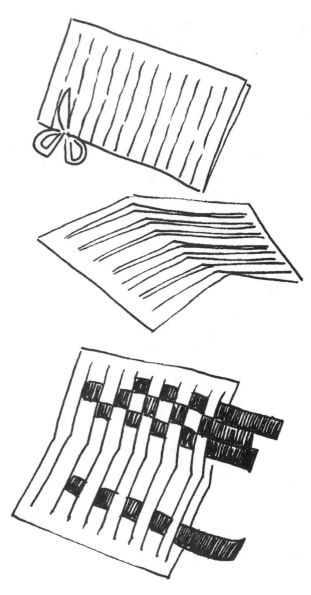

Weaving Mats

Chapter
25

Fun Around the World for Preschoolers

In The United States

United States

ALASKA
Alaska in Pictures
In advance, gather pictures of things seen in Alaska, such as snow-capped mountains, brown bears, polar bears, whales, glacier, moose, bald eagles, and seals.

Lead preschoolers to help you mount the pictures on pieces of construction paper. Bind the pages together to make a book. Print the title Alaska in Pictures.

Shadow Book
Materials: white paper, black construction paper, scissors, shadow patterns, hole punch, yarn, self-sealing bag or an envelope, hook-and-loop fastener

Cut shadow pictures out of black construction paper by enlarging and reproducing the patterns to the left. Mount the shadow pictures on white paper, then fold pages in half. Punch two holes and tie yarn through to hold the pages together. Put a hook-and-loop fastener piece on each pattern and each shadow. Store pattern pieces in the envelope or self-sealing bag in the back of the book.

Print under each shadow *I live in Alaska. What am I?* Suggest boys and girls match each picture with its shadow.

The Polar Bear Jump
Materials: large piece of fabric or area carpet

Tell preschoolers that some of the people in Seward, Alaska, participate in The Polar Bear Jump. People jump into the icy cold water of Resurrection Bay to raise money for charity groups. Explain that the fabric or carpet represents Resurrection Bay. Tell preschoolers to stand around the edge of the water. Say: 1-2-3. Jump!

Allow preschoolers to jump into the "water." Repeat the activity with varying challenges: Jump in on one foot. Jump in while holding a friend's hand. Jump in backwards, etc.

Icebergs
Materials: water table or plastic dishpan, bowls, picture of a glacier, plastic arctic animals

In advance, fill containers with water and freeze them.

Remove frozen ice from bowls and put them in the water in the water table or dishpan. Add the plastic arctic animals. Say: Some parts of Alaska are so cold that ice forms, making a glacier. The big pieces of glaciers that fall into the water are called icebergs.

Shadow Book

Icebergs

Colorful Mittens

Materials: construction paper, mitten pattern, crayons, markers, glue, sequins, fabric scraps, scissors, yarn, hole punch

In advance, photocopy the pattern at right for each child.

Assist each preschooler as he traces his pattern onto the construction paper. Help each child cut two mittens from the construction paper. Guide preschoolers to decorate their mittens using the art supplies. Punch a hole at the top of each mitten and string yarn through the holes to make each child a set of mittens. Say: Winters are very cold in Alaska. Mittens help keep hands warm.

Browsing the Books

Transform a corner of the room into a winter cave. A large appliance box works well. Place a sign near the entrance that reads *Snuggle up with a good book.* Decorate the cave to look like it is covered with snow. Add a few warm blankets. Provide a variety of age-appropriate books related to Alaska. Encourage preschoolers to crawl in the box and relax while reading a good book.

Colorful Mittens

CALIFORNIA

A California Town

Materials: green, black, red, yellow felt; scissors; miniature toy vehicles; box

In advance, cut a piece of green felt large enough to cover a tabletop. Cut black felt strips to resemble roads. Cut out felt trees and buildings. Store the felt pieces in a box.

Guide preschoolers to set up a town using the felt pieces. Say: Many cities and towns are in California.

The Basket Is Empty

Guide preschoolers to form a circle. Choose one child to stand in the middle holding a basket. As the others sing, ask the child in the middle to pretend to fill the basket while doing the actions. Sing to the tune "Did You Ever See a Lassie?":

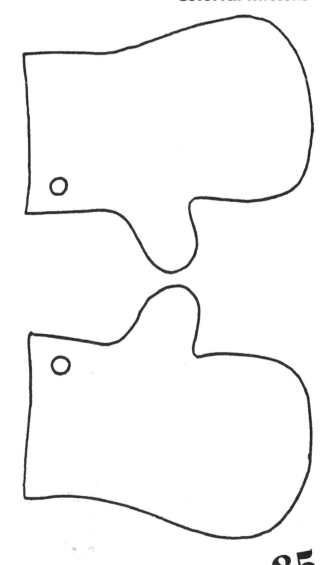

Did you ever fill a basket, a basket, a basket?
Did you ever fill a basket with apples like this?
(Pretends to pick apples)
Pick them this way and that way,
and this way and that way.
Did you ever fill a basket with apples like this?

Did you ever fill a basket, a basket, a basket?
Did you ever fill a basket with sand like this?
Scoop it this way and that way,
and this way and that way.
Did you ever fill a basket with sand like this?

Island Table Mat

Melting Crayons

Continue suggesting actions and giving others an opportunity to be in the middle. Encourage the boys and girls to think of ways to fill the basket. Say: Lots of fruits and vegetables grow in California. How do you think the farmer gets the fruit and vegetables to market?

HAWAII

Island Table Mat
Cover a table with white butcher paper. Display a picture of the Hawaiian Islands. Lead preschoolers to help you draw islands on the paper. Work together to color the islands green and the water blue. Provide toy cars, boats, airplanes, and use small blocks for houses. Encourage preschoolers to fly, sail, and drive on and between the islands.

Teaching Tip: Accuracy is not important when preschoolers help you draw.

Melting Crayons
Materials: food-warming tray, foil, electrical outlet, typing paper, crayons (with paper removed), pencil

Plug in the food-warming tray. Cover the tray top with foil. Invite preschoolers to place a sheet of paper on the tray. Show how to hold the crayons at the top and move slowly along the paper, letting the crayon melt onto the paper. Encourage preschoolers to work together to fill the whole page. Older preschoolers can draw colorful fish and fill around them with blue water. Say: Hawaii is a beautiful state with a rainbow of colors and fish.

Teaching Tip: Make it easier to remove paper from crayons by soaking them in water.

Caution: Supervise carefully when preschoolers are near the warm tray.

Dressing up Aloha Style
Place a variety of aloha clothing (leis, muumuus, swimsuits, shirts, shorts, sandals, beach towels, hats, sunglasses) in the area. Display a picture of boys and girls wearing aloha clothes. Encourage preschoolers to dress-up Hawaiian style. Say: Most people in Hawaii, even guests, dress in aloha clothes.

Note: Aloha clothes are made with tropical, floral fabric in a rainbow of colors.

Beach-Ball Toss
Suspend hula hoops from the ceiling. Inflate several beach balls. Play Hawaiian music as preschoolers toss the balls through the hoops. Say: Hawaiian people enjoy listening and moving to music.

Hawaiian Alphabet

Beginning readers will enjoy seeing how small the Hawaiian alphabet is. Print the letters *A, E, H, I, K, L, M, N, O P, U,* and *W* on a large piece of paper. With preschoolers, count the letters and compare to our alphabet. Invite preschoolers to copy letters, make a list of words that begin with some of the letters, or say the names of the letters. Say: The Hawaiian alphabet has only 12 letters! Is that larger or smaller than our alphabet?

Airplane Ride

Materials: masking tape, chairs, cart with toy food and cups, tickets made from index cards, suitcases or backpacks, magazines for reading, leis

In advance, make a large airplane-cabin shape on the floor with masking tape. Add rows of chairs inside the plane, including a place for pilots and flight attendants. Stow the food cart at the back of the plane.

Invite preschoolers to board a flight to Hawaii. Let each have a ticket, bring a bag, and get on the plane. Take turns being the pilot, flight attendant, and passengers. Suggest one child serve the passengers a snack. Lead others to read magazines during the flight. Upon arrival in Hawaii, greet each passenger with a flower lei, and say: Aloha! Welcome to our tropical island.

Sugarcane, Pineapple, and Coffee

Place a piece of *ko* [KOH] which means sugarcane in Hawaiian, and sugar in a bowl; a pineapple and a can of pineapple, coffee beans, and ground coffee on a table. Post the allergy alert chart (p. 93). With preschoolers, look at each item, comparing how they are changed to be ready for people to use them. Say: These items grow in Hawaii.

ILLINOIS

The Sears Tower

Tell preschoolers that Chicago is home of the tallest building in North America, the Sears Tower. Encourage preschoolers to build a tall building with soft foam blocks.

Taste of Chicago

Materials: ethnic plastic play foods; ethnic props (chopsticks, woks, piñata, etc.)

Help preschoolers role-play the Taste of Chicago, an annual event where ethnic foods are displayed and sold at Grant Park in Chicago. Say: Many people come to Grant Park to taste the food.

Airplane Ride

Sugarcane, Pineapple, and Coffee

Handprint Zoo Animals

Handprint Zoo Animals

Materials: fabric scraps, paper, crayons and markers, paint, sponges (for painting), scissors, glue, leaves, grass

Help preschoolers trace their hands on light colored paper. Allow them to use the materials to create the markings and features of their favorite zoo animals on their hand tracings. Encourage them to create the animals' natural environment with the leaves and grass.

Say: Chicago is home to the world's largest free public zoo.

Apartment Buildings and Houses

Materials: variety of empty food boxes covered in butcher paper, empty spools and film canisters, toy vehicles, people figures

Encourage interested preschoolers to build a city with apartment buildings and houses. Say: Chicago is a large city. Many people live in its apartments and houses.

LOUISIANA

Metal Music

Place several metal spoons and metal tins on the floor. Invite preschoolers to make music by tapping spoons on the tins. Compare the sounds from different sized tins. Say: Louisiana is famous for its jazz music.

Life on the River

Lead preschoolers on a pretend trip on the Mississippi River. Climb into a boat, and begin to row. Row and move down river. Stop and climb out. Go for a swim in the water. Fish for some lunch. Get back in the boat and row home.

Help preschoolers use their imaginations. Say: Look at the raccoon. The trees are beautiful. Many people enjoy sightseeing on the Mississippi River.

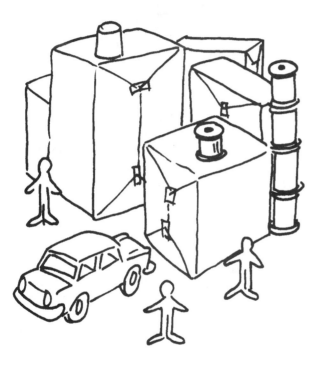

Apartment Buildings and Houses

MICHIGAN

Tasting Apples

Materials: knife; paper plates; apples (yellow, red, green); allergy alert chart (p. 93)

Post the chart to notify parents of this activity. Wash the fruit and display. Ask preschoolers to identify the different colored apples. Give them a choice as to which one they would like to taste.

Say: The state flower of Michigan is the apple blossom. Apple blossoms make apples. We can eat this fruit raw, or we can cook it and make apple pies or cakes. Apples are a healthy snack.

Older babies and toddlers will enjoy tasting applesauce.

Toddlers and younger preschoolers will enjoy a snack of o-shaped cereal. Say: Grain is grown in Michigan. Grain is made into cereal and bread. Grain is a healthy food.

Easel Painting

Materials: easel, watercolors, paper, brushes, large shirts to cover preschoolers' clothing

Place a protective shirt on each child as he arrives in the Art area. Guide preschoolers to dip the brushes in containers of paint and wipe off the excess before placing on the paper. Say: Michigan is a beautiful state. It has big forests and many lakes. Ships bring food and other items through canals from the Atlantic Ocean. Would you like to paint a picture of something you might see in Michigan?

If an easel is unavailable, place drawing paper on tables.

Teaching Tip: Offer sincere praise for a child's efforts.

Riding a Snowmobile

Materials: unit blocks, riding toys such as a tricycle

Form a long path by using unit blocks. Say: Riding snowmobiles is a favorite winter sport in Michigan. Many tourists come to the state to ride snowmobiles. We will pretend your tricycle is a snowmobile we are riding on a path. We will have fun playing with our friends.

Caution: Closely supervise the use of the tricycle.

Snow Play

Materials: unit blocks, small area rugs

Younger preschoolers will enjoy building with unit blocks. Guide them to stack several blocks together. Say: Children play in the snow in Michigan. They build objects from snow. Let's build a snow house with blocks.

Place the rugs inside the snow house. Encourage preschoolers to work together on this group project.

MONTANA

Footprints in the Snow

Materials: white tempera paint on a paper plate, blue construction paper, aprons

After putting on aprons, let preschoolers dip their fingers in paint and finger walk across the paper. Encourage them to make white prints on the paper. Say: Lots of snow falls in Montana.

Backpacking Trip

Materials: backpack, hiking boots, hat, sunglasses, play food items, empty water bottle, towel, compass, binoculars, walking stick

Display a picture of people hiking in the mountains or woods. Help a preschooler get ready for a hiking trip. Talk about hiker needs. Say: Visitors go to hike in Montana.

Easel Painting

Snow Play

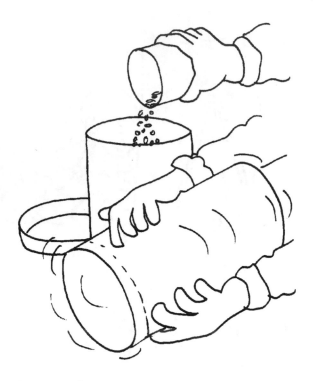

Oatmeal Swoosh Can

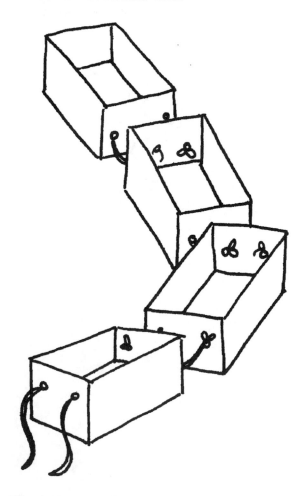

Shoe-Box Train

Oatmeal Swoosh Can

Guide preschoolers to help you fill empty oatmeal can with 1 cup of raw rice. Secure the lid with duct tape. Cover the can with white paper. Ask preschoolers to glue pictures of skis and snowflakes onto the can. Show preschoolers how to hold the swoosh can horizontal to their bodies, and slowly and gently swoosh it from side to side. Say: Listen to the sound the rice makes. Skiers in Montana make a swoosh sound when they ski.

Sparkly Play Dough

Use the recipe on page 76 to make play dough. Instead of food coloring, add iridescent glitter to the dry ingredients. Help preschoolers build snowmen, snowballs, and igloos. Say: People play in the snow in Montana.

NEW YORK
International Flavor

Post the allergy alert chart on page 93 to notify parents of this tasting activity.

Provide snacks from different ethnic groups for preschoolers to taste. Matzo bread (Jewish), Chinese noodles, tortillas, and pasta dishes are just a few suggestions.

As preschoolers enjoy the snacks, say: People from many different countries live in New York City.

Shoe-Box Train

Materials: three or four shoe boxes (no lids), nylon twine, small toys, blocks

In advance, punch a hole in each end of the shoe boxes. Join shoe boxes together with 8 lengths of nylon twine. Knot twine to hold in place or tape to the inside of the box.

Place the train in the area. Encourage preschoolers to fill the train boxes with blocks or small toys to transport to another area. Say: New York City has many kinds of trains that carry things around. Some trains carry people, some carry food, some carry equipment builders need. Trains carry many different things.

OREGON
One Scoop or Two?

Materials: empty ice cream cartons, scoops, cone-shaped coffee filters, colored pom-poms, aprons, note pad, pencil, sponge to clean counter, toy cash register

In advance, make a chart listing the ice cream flavors.

Guide boys and girls to take turns taking orders for ice cream, serving the ice cream, collecting the money, and eating the ice cream. Say: As people travel through Oregon, they see dairy farms. The cows produce milk that is used to make ice cream.

Travel Guide

Materials: paper; nature pictures of cows, flowers, water-falls, a beach, mountains, lighthouse; clear plastic holders; notebook

Make the same number of pages for the travel guide as the number of pictures. Glue one picture on each page. Print under each picture what can be seen in Oregon, such as *See the mountains in Oregon.*

Traveling Through Oregon

Lead preschoolers in the following movement activity.

I can travel in an airplane.
I can fly low, I can fly high, I can fly all
around seeing the beautiful things in Oregon.

I can travel in a car.
I can drive up and down the roads and around the
curves,
just so I can see the beautiful things in Oregon.

I can travel in a dune buggy.
I can drive on the sand and go down to the ocean
while I am seeing the beautiful things in Oregon.

I can travel in a boat out on the water.
I can sail right on by the fish and crabs.
I might see a whale swim by
as I am looking for beautiful things to see in Oregon.

Travel Guide

TEXAS

The Metroplex

Materials: wooden blocks, people figures, toy vehicles, transportation theme area rug or floor mat

Place the rug or mat on the floor. Invite interested pre-schoolers to help you build a large city with buildings, streets, vehicles, and people. Say: The Dallas/Fort Worth Metroplex is in Texas. It has many, many people. Many students go to middle school and high school in the Dallas/Fort Worth area.

Remind preschoolers to use the blocks to build a pre-tend school where the students go to learn.

Postcard Book

In advance, make a postcard book using postcards purchased or collected that show scenes from the Dallas/Fort Worth area. Place all the postcards on a metal ring.

Flip through the postcards and talk about the pictures with preschoolers.

Teaching Tip: If you do not have postcards, visit a travel agency and collect brochures or flyers with pictures of the area. Or check the Internet for photos of the area.

The Metroplex

Airplane Flying

Airplane Flying

Say: The Dallas/Fort Worth area has a large airport.

Teach preschoolers this action rhyme to the tune of "I'm a Little Teapot":

I'm a little airplane, (Raise arms at sides to shoulder height.)

Now watch me fly! (Spin one arm in front as if it were a propeller.)

Here are my instruments from low to up high. (With the other arm, reach from the ground to above heads.)

First I get all revved up. (Make engine-like noises while still spinning their arms.)

Then I can fly, (Raise arms to shoulder height.)

Lifting off the runway (Start walking forward.)

Up into the sky! (Go up on tiptoes and continue to move forward.)

Let preschoolers circle a while before returning to their original positions.

WASHINGTON

Play-Dough Sculptures

Prepare play dough using the recipe on page 76. Place play dough, craft sticks, buttons, pieces of ribbon, chenille stems, and paper plates on a table.

Invite preschoolers to make a sculpture with play dough. Let them add other items to their sculptures. Dry on paper plates. Say: Many sculptures are in the Puget Sound area of Washington. People enjoy looking at sculptures.

Coffee Shop

Materials: coffee cups, coffeepot (metal), napkins, apron, play money, toy cookies and doughnuts

Make a triangle with two tables and the homeliving kitchen, forming a coffee bar. Place chairs along the bar. Invite preschoolers to come to the coffee shop. Lead preschoolers to take turns wearing an apron and pretending to be the coffee server. Say: Many people in Washington enjoy going to coffee shops or stands. Drinking coffee is popular.

Allergy Alert Chart

Look what preschoolers are doing!

We will _____

_____

_____

_____

_____

_____

If your child is allergic to any of these items, please sign his/her name below.

Child's Name

_____

_____

_____

_____

Allergic to

_____

_____

_____

_____

Photocopy and laminate to reuse. Use a grease pencil or washable marker to note items used in a session.

Notes

Notes

Notes

Notes

Notes

Notes

Notes

Notes

Notes

Notes

Also in the
FUN
AROUND THE
WORLD
series, written for first-through sixth-graders.

Fun Around the World
1-56309-052-X

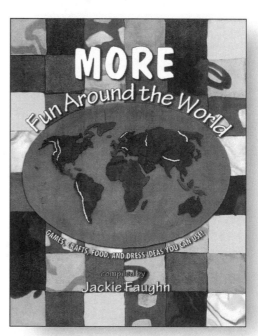

More Fun Around the World
1-56309-260-3

Available in Christian bookstores everywhere.

new
hope
PUBLISHERS

Inspiring Women. Changing Lives.